A CHRISTIAN PERSPECTIVE

The Employed Wife

Earning a Living, Making a Home

Lenore Buth

Copyright © 1986 Concordia Publishing House
3558 S. Jefferson Avenue, St. Louis, MO 63118-3968
Manufactured in the United States of America

Library of Congress Cataloging in Publication Data

Buth, Lenore.
    The employed wife.

      1. Wives—Psychology. 2. Wives—Employment. 3. Working mothers. 4. Wives—Religious life.
I. Title.
HQ759.B829 1987   306.8'7   86-12908
ISBN 0-570-04436-7

2 3 4 5 6 7 8 9 10   95

The Employed Wife

To every woman who "has it all"—
who continuously wears at least two hats:
   paid worker
   wife
   mother
   single parent
   chief cook and bottle-washer
   (and who is probably exhausted)
   I salute you!

Contents

Preface

Want to try an experiment? Bring up the question whether married women, with or without children, should work outside the home for pay. Casually introduce the subject to Christians or non-Christians. No matter where or when you broach the topic, you're almost guaranteed a spirited discussion.

Like everyone else, I have my personal bias. It seems to me that perhaps we as a society discount the importance of mothering. In my ideal world, every mother could decide (without pressure) whether or not to be at home with her children. Circumstances, however, are seldom ideal. Nevertheless, I think it's vital that parents carefully weigh the cost as well as the benefits when analyzing potential net gain from the wife's income. A price tag may be attached that is higher than you'd noticed.

Whatever one's individual opinion may be, the fact is that every day more married women—Christian women, too—join the millions already employed outside the home. A large percentage are mothers of young children. Many are reluctantly forced into that choice because of genuine financial need. (In case you're wondering, the Bible doesn't specifically address living out the dual-career marriage.)

On these pages you won't find a definitive argument either for or against the two-paycheck life-style. That's a decision for each couple individually. Because the everyday challenges of building a strong marriage are intensified when both partners are employed, we'll examine some of the stresses on the relationship. And we'll look for practical applications of Scriptural principles.

I'm indebted to the many dual-career couples who shared their insights when answering my survey. Many of the quotes used are theirs; others are a composite of comments, snatches of countless conversations, plus a bit of my own invention. In all cases, names and details are fictional and no resemblance to particular individuals is intended.

This book has only one aim: to strengthen the reader as a Christian and as a marriage partner/parent. Whether you're coping and confident, or stumbling and struggling, you do not walk alone. The Lord your God is there beside you!

I lift up my eyes to the hills—
    where does my help come from?
My help comes from the Lord,
    the Maker of heaven and earth.

He will not let your foot slip—
    he who watches over you will not slumber;
indeed, he who watches over Israel
    will neither slumber nor sleep.

The Lord watches over you—
    the Lord is your shade at your right hand;
The sun will not harm you by day,
    nor the moon by night.

The Lord will keep you from all harm—
    he will watch over your life;
the Lord will watch over your coming and going
    both now and forevermore.

Psalm 121

1
The Many Faces of Freedom

I feel like a juggler, always trying to keep too many balls in the air at the same time. Jugglers, however, get to stop and rest now and then.
    —*Wife*

Sure, it's hectic running my own business, but I love every minute of it! Jack and I are true partners; we share everything—the cooking and cleanup, the child care and the time off. I've never been happier, and I think Jack would say the same.
    —*Wife*

My kids are really good little troopers. They realize I can't get time off to come to their school programs and ball games. In fact, they don't even ask any more. Sometimes, though, they let their guard down and I see their hurt. Times like that I want to cry for all of us. Sometimes I do.
    —*Wife*

If I'd been born a generation ago, I'd never have had a chance to become a fire fighter—and I love it!
    —*Wife*

It's pretty clear to me that I come in second—and maybe not even that. Sharon brings work home, the baby cries, the dog barfs, whatever . . . I can always wait. Most of our fights are about this, and she always promises her usual promises. Then the next time something comes up, she says, "I'm sorry, Jon, but I know you understand." But I am tired of understanding!
    —Husband

Every cell in my body screams, 'Burnout!' That last promotion put me over the edge. I'm proud of what I've accomplished and I'm earning more money than ever before. But my responsibilities have increased in direct proportion. Still, I'm not ready to give up the life-style my income provides us. And even though Will complains, neither is he.
    —Wife

How about you? When you consider your own life as a wife/mother/wage-earner, do you feel enriched or enslaved? Do you consider yourself an equal partner in your marriage or the prisoner of a system you didn't design?

There is no "typical working wife." *All* wives and mothers work. Yet the phrase "working wife" has come to mean the married woman who earns a wage, usually outside the home.

Second, the motivations and satisfaction levels of working women vary as much as the women themselves—from career dedication to economic necessity to escape from boredom. For every working wife who relishes her emancipation from the four walls of home, there's another who yearns to be provided for by an old-fashioned husband. For every mother who's glad to escape diapers and baby talk, there's another who sheds a tear every morning as she hands over her child to the care and control of someone else.

There seem to be two common factors, however: too little time and a sense of underlying fatigue. No matter how invigorating the job, most working wives feel stressed. As Rosemary puts it, "It takes all you've got—and then some!"

Good scheduling helps, of course. Yet that tight, efficient time schedule can become a tyrant. Pulled between your work, your husband, and your children, time for yourself becomes a scarce commodity. That adds to the tension, for all of us need solitary time—time that's *not* "productive"—in order to maintain our emotional equilibrium. In fact, that "wasted" time is often most productive of all.

Nevertheless, there are exceptions. Perhaps you know a woman who seems able to manage her triple role of wife, mother, and worker without effort. "If she can do it and not be frazzled," you ask yourself, "why can't I?"

Instead of comparing yourself to such an exotic species, face the fact that you're likely a garden-variety mortal. So relax and accept yourself—and your situation. Concentrate on what you are rather than on what you lack.

That's the first requisite for survival and sanity. The second is even more important. In fact, if you want to navigate smoothly over the choppy seas of this life-style, don't set sail without it.

The Source of True Freedom

Caught in the midst of the constant demands and expectations of others, wives and mothers often feel anything but free. Nevertheless, we live in what's often called "the age of personal freedom," because many racial and sexual barriers have been abolished. Logically, that should afford satisfaction and serenity.

Yet removal of employment restraints doesn't appear to have ushered in emotional peace. Stress and depression are epidemic throughout the population. Nor is freedom the sure companion to a wide range of options. In fact, some of the people who are most unfettered in their hearts and minds lead severely restricted lives.

True freedom arises from within.

The key is to start there. To use a slang expression, first make sure that your own head is on straight. A life founded on fluff won't get you through your challenging days. You need a solid core—the inner security that comes from knowing who you are. Despite the whirl of conflicting opinion, regardless of newscasters prophesying destruction, you can have an unshakable center. God's free gifts to His children are yours. Life now (John 6:35; 10:10) and life eternal (John 3:16), true freedom (John 8:31–32, 36), peace (Rom. 5:1), inner strength (Eph. 3:14–17)—all are yours in Christ.

Free to Be Human

*L*iving faith in Christ gives us a foundation that doesn't crack and crumble when the going gets rough—or stays rough.

"I'm so tired of being strong!" says Jessie. "At work I dare not betray any emotion or admit my weakness, or I'll be perceived as a 'typical female'—and that's the kiss of death. In our company you can be a woman, but you have to be a woman who acts like a man if you want to move up the ladder.

"At home I have to be strong, too. If Paul thinks I can't handle my schedule, he'll feel guilty for taking time off from his job to get his doctorate. So . . . it's stiff-upper-lip all the way.

"I am proud to be capable," Jessie continues. "But there's never an opportunity to kick back and shift into neutral. Know what I mean? It's just keep on keeping on. Even with his degree, Paul will never earn enough in his field so that I can quit work. This is for life . . . and that overwhelms me."

Jessie has many sisters—women who feel compelled to outperform male co-workers so that they'll be taken seriously. Women expected to hold up more than their share, on the job and in the home—perhaps that's your situation.

The good news is that as you run your daily marathon, you're not alone. You have a Helper (Ps. 121:2). The apostle Paul promised that God will meet all your needs (Phil. 4:19)—and that includes strengthening you to cope with your daily routine.

Burn that into your consciousness. Repeat it over and over to yourself. Center your thoughts on the unlimited power of God Almighty. Then you can tackle with quiet confidence whatever comes.

Free to Accept Ourselves

The apostle Paul knew his own limitations well, and he was nobody's fool. He faced constant, formidable opposition from within and without. Although a reading of 2 Cor. 11:23–33 gives us a glimpse of the hardships he endured and might lead us to judge him superhuman, Paul took the opposite view. He not only recognized his own weaknesses and handicaps—he delighted in them (2 Cor. 12:7–10).

Paul chose to take his mysterious "thorn in the flesh," an unidentified physical problem, and the ordeals he faced as reminders that drove him back to God, the source of strength. Paul's inability to cope on his own forced him to rely on God. And God, who *is* able, brought Paul through every tribulation—bloodied, perhaps, but unbowed.

To paraphrase the old saying, Paul worked as if everything depended on his own efforts. But he prayed, praised, and thanked God as if everything depended on the Lord. And he trusted God with the outcome. (For most of us, that latter point is the real stickler.)

Free to Flourish Where You Are

Your own life may be less than thrilling right now. Your weeks may, in fact, be a succession of days in which you'd love to sit down and bawl, only "big girls don't cry"—especially those who want to get anywhere on the job.

So it's vital to keep in mind that *Paul's God is our God!* He is faithful—yesterday, today, tomorrow (Ps. 117; Heb. 13:8; Rev. 1:8; 22:13). Yet you may have asked Him repeatedly to change your life circumstances; to transform your unfeeling employer; to replace that backbiting opportunist across the aisle into a supportive friend; to bring forth a loving, reliable person for child care. (Maybe even that one day you'll receive an unexpected windfall hefty enough to allow you more choices.) Nothing changes, however. Where, you wonder, is God? Doesn't He care?

Don't worry. God wants only your good (Matt. 7:7–11). The catch is that His timetable, His aim, and His methods probably differ from your own.

Free to Be Shaped

*I*t's clear that one of God's ongoing purposes is that we grow to be more like Christ. To accomplish that, He often uses situations, people, and places we wouldn't choose. So, for example, He may allow us to remain where we are, though we desperately long to escape.

To be sure, it would be pleasant (and impressive) if He simply whisked us out of the problem. But how much more useful it is in the long run, when God molds us and changes us *where we are!* After all, this may not be our last aggravation.

Consider the benefits, once we come out on the other side: more self-confidence and better coping skills, because we hadn't just cut and run; stronger faith, because we'd seen God at work. Most of the time, getting from here to there is a slow metamorphosis, so gradual that we're unaware of the alterations while they're under way. It's only later, when we look back, that we can gauge our progress.

When we trust God's direction and all-sufficiency, we're free to take our eyes off ourselves and just do what needs to be done. No sweat, because the burden of responsibility rests with our heavenly Father. That subtracts nothing from us except tension. It is, in fact, God's prescription for that feeling of constant pressure.

It's important to emphasize that no one's suggesting that you must become a limp dishrag (Rom. 8:15–17), nor that you give up decision making. The apostle Paul was hardly powerless and unassertive. Rather, he maintained a right perspective on the relationship between God and himself:

God is the Creator; human beings are His creation (Ps. 100:3). Paul never lost sight of that, so God could use him mightily. That's also the secret of Paul's unperturbed, optimistic response to continuing opposition and persecution (Rom. 8:35–39; 2 Cor. 1:3–10).

Free to Trust

*I*t appears that Paul had little leisure, or even discretionary time. Yet he didn't burn out. The peace that passes all understanding (Phil. 4:4–7) was Paul's secret. It came because Paul was abiding in Christ and Christ in Paul (John 15:1–5). He believed Christ's commands and promises, and he went a step farther. He lived as if they were true, seeing himself as merely the instrument through which Christ would work. Paul wasn't intimidated by anything or anyone. He said:

> I have learned the secret of being content in any and every situation. . . . I can do everything through him who gives me strength. (Phil. 4:12–13)

Nevertheless, it's hard for us to adopt what seems to be a passive stance. Most of us have definite opinions as to how our lives ought to proceed. What we really want is for God to rubber-stamp our requests "Approved" and then to send them through—pronto. Think about the phraseology we typically use in our prayers: "Lord, please let—" "Lord, please make—" "Lord, help me to—"

Sometimes we dictate rather than pray. That shouldn't surprise us, for achievers pride themselves on ordering their own lives. In this self-help age, we customarily weigh the alternatives, set our goals, plan how to implement them and then get to work. We are actors, not reactors. We pay our dues—and we're usually rather pleased with ourselves.

Perhaps you've carefully honed your self-sufficiency, so talk of relinquishing control—to anyone—makes alarm bells ring in your brain.

"Look," says Ramona, "I've worked hard to get where I am. I used to be a doormat. No more! I'm proud of what I've become and what I've accomplished. I am a take-charge lady, and I like that. I love the Lord, and I think I trust Him. But you may as well be talking a foreign language. . . . I haven't a clue even how to begin—and frankly, I'm not sure I want to!"

If you feel like Ramona, square one is to ask God to show you what He would have *you* to do. Ask Him to make you willing to change. As time goes on, the Holy Spirit will gently show you the way and lead you (John 14:26; Rom. 8:26–27). And have no fear. Although none of us knows the way ahead, we can live in assurance. For we walk hand-in-hand with the One who created us and scheduled every second of yesterday, today, and tomorrow (Ps. 139).

Free to Keep On Growing

As a Christian, I believe it's important to have a strong faith," says Dana. "I see that my kids are in Sunday school, and we worship together as a family each Sunday. The crunch comes in trying to handle all my responsibilities and not short-change anyone. To be honest, I'm not sure religion is terribly relevant to my daily life. I need practical tips to help me manage my life, not philosophical concepts!"

Isn't it interesting how we compartmentalize ourselves and our lives? Yet Jesus never did. For instance, He told us to love God with all our heart, with all our soul, and with all our mind (Matt. 22:37). We are whole persons, and our lives, too, are all of a piece.

Besides, "religion" can denote any system of beliefs. Christianity is more than that. Christianity is a living relationship with the living Lord. That love relationship, as close as that of a branch growing out of the Vine, is intended to color everything we do every day. When we relegate faith to a "feel-good" hour on Sunday morning, we're settling for crumbs when we could have a banquet.

In the frenetic, fully committed lives we lead, we urgently need a stabilizer. All the good advice we read—on the value of relaxation, exercise, recreation, etc.—can be helpful in maintaining balance. But the job can't be done from the outside in. Rather, what's inside us dictates how (whether) we'll meet the demands of our double lives.

That makes our most important task to nurture the spiritual core of our beings. We feed our bodies healthy food. We nourish our skin with exotic creams. Our spirits need regular sustenance, too.

Free to Grow Spiritually

When you list your activities for the day, commit some time to read the Bible and to let God speak to your heart. (The most necessary ingredient in "finding" time is your own mind-set to do so.) When and how is up to you. Some people get up early to have a quiet time before the daily clamor begins. Others can't concentrate until much later in the day. Some use undisturbed time while riding public transportation to work or time during their lunch hours. Other prefer to read the Bible just before retiring, so they can fall asleep with God's Word fresh in their minds.

Use one of the newer translations for easier comprehension, such as the New International Version or Today's English Version. You don't need a study guide. Just begin by asking God the Holy Spirit to help you understand. If you're unfamiliar with the Bible, you may want to begin with a part of the New Testament, such as the Gospel of John. Then move on to Paul's epistles. In any case, it's better to read a small section with thought and understanding than to race through several chapters.

Reread and take a few minutes to reflect on what you've covered. Or dig a little deeper. For instance, read the verses once for general content. Then go over them again, asking yourself, "How does this apply to me and my life?" Again, allow time to consider that section and the applications that come to mind. You might want to keep a small notebook and jot down what you find most meaningful.

As you mine the riches of God's written Word, you can count on Him to bless your faithfulness (Ps. 119:11; Is. 55:10–11; Luke 11:28; Rom. 10:17; 15:4; 2 Tim. 3:15–17). Occasionally you'll miss a day on your spiritual diet. You are, after all, human. The same advice applies here as on a food diet: Forgive yourself, pick it up again, and go on.

Tuck a small Bible or New Testament in your handbag to read while you wait for an appointment. Enrich your life, rather than "kill time." Commentaries are useful. But it is often better to read the Bible prayerfully first and draw out personal applications. *Then* read a commentary.

Free to Talk to God

*T*alk to your heavenly Father in prayer, too. One logical choice of time is after reading His Word; you can focus your thoughts by meditating on what you've just read. But any time will do.

Think about God—who He is as well as what He does/has done—and praise Him for it. Confess your sins and failures to Him. Thank Him that the blood of His Son, Jesus Christ, washes your sins away and gives you a fresh start. Thank Him for His blessings—past, present, and future. Allow some times of silence and let the Holy Spirit bring to mind people and situations for which to pray.

Even persons with tightly packed schedules can make time for prayer—if they choose to. You can pray while you jog or walk. You can commit your day to the Lord in those first moments of wakefulness before you arise. Some who drive to work alone make Jesus their "traveling companion." Some of them say aloud what's on their hearts as they commute to and from work. (If other drivers notice your lips moving, they'll assume you're singing along with the radio.) While standing in line or waiting for the copier to crank out your material, "tune out" your surroundings and pray silently. Send silent "arrow prayers" (brief and to the point) during tense business conferences.

The point is not where, when, or how. God isn't concerned with precise rituals but with the sincerity of our hearts (1 Sam. 16:7; Ps. 51:10) and minds (Is. 26:3). He desires our fellowship, and we're dependent on His. As with those whom we love, if we want to maintain our relationship, we accord it priority status. That requires time. It means openness and honesty—not only talking but also listening.

Regular communication with our Creator nourishes us spiritually, as He renews us and restores us to a healthy perspective. The circumstances of our life may not alter a bit, but we'll be less stressed within. And that's no small gift!

Free to Find Rest

*L*ook," says Rosemary, "I told you before that I already can't manage all I'm expected to do. How in the world am I supposed to 'find' the time—and the energy—for all this? Yes, I know it's worthwhile, but come on, let's be realistic!"

Perhaps you agree. You're pushed to your limit as it is. Just one more "should," one more "ought to," and you'll go over the edge.

Most of us know that feeling. Good resolutions (unfulfilled) litter our days. Disposable time is almost nil, so we deal in "have to" tasks. Predictably, we come through for the person who'll lean over us on Monday morning and ask, "How are you coming?" and for family members, whose very presence each day nudges us to come through.

God, on the other hand, is patient. We take it for granted that He'll forgive us for Christ's sake and love us, no matter how often we fail. We live under grace—and we can't see His imploring eyes.

So days—weeks—go by, and we frantically race through our maze of responsibilities at work and at home. We down endless cups of coffee and pop aspirin, pep pills, and/or tranquilizers, struggling to make it through our days, never caught up, never coming to a resting place for our bodies, much less our souls. Yet what we long for most is rest.

Jesus said:

Come to me, all you who are weary and burdened, and I will give you rest. Take my yoke upon you and learn from me, for I am gentle and humble in heart, and you will find rest for your souls. For my yoke is easy and my burden is light. (Matthew 11:28–30)

He who is our Enabler promises to be our Rest. His yoke (of learning and of acknowledging Him Lord) is easy because it fits perfectly; in fact, we were created to wear it. The burden (obligations of discipleship) is light, for He supplies the strength to bear it, and through it He blesses us in ways we couldn't foresee.

Christ's words remain fresh and timeless. After all, our modern value system is just the same old value system, wearing designer clothes. Matt. 6:19–34 perfectly describes us, dwellers in this Age of Acquisition. Christ clearly sets down His priority system in verses 31–33:

> So do not worry, saying, "What shall we eat?" or "What shall we drink?" or "What shall we wear?" For the pagans run after all these things, and your heavenly Father knows that you need them. But seek first his kingdom and his righteousness, and all these things will be given to you as well.

That doesn't mean that life's daily necessities come to the Christian without effort. Whatever our responsibilities, at work or at home, as Christ's followers we're to be honest and faithful, to carry out our tasks with commitment and diligence and as unto the Lord.

Free to Light the Way

*L*ived out in practical terms, that life-style will set us apart from the crowd.

"I've never known anyone like Carolyn," says Barb. "Even when everything in her life seems to be falling apart, she stays calm—and she's always optimistic. I asked her once how she can be 'up' all the time, when the world is in such a mess. She just smiled and said, 'Oh, I don't worry. The same God who made the world is in charge of today—and of tomorrow. And I just trust Him, rather than the headlines.'

"Honestly," Barb continues, "Carolyn is . . . different. Like when a bit of juicy gossip comes along, she stays out of it. In fact, Carolyn usually finds something good to say. And she's a real people person—always helping somebody out. Pulls her fair share around here, too, and then some. Maybe I'm making her sound like a super saintly type, but she's not. She's so down to earth and so ready to let other people get the credit that everybody likes her. And trusts her . . . that lady is 100 percent honest—bet she's never even taken home a paper clip. I tell you, that Carolyn Smith is a rare bird!"

Christians like Carolyn Smith telegraph that they're rooted in Christ, for the fruits of the Spirit are plain to see. Your own busy schedule may limit your involvement at church. Nevertheless, you can be in ministry every day by living out your Christian faith. Co-workers *will* notice. Then one day, when they ask what makes you different, they'll be ready to listen.

Your personal commitment could be a powerful influence in your workplace. Some years ago, a woman who worked for an international firm began silently reading her Bible as she ate her brown-bag lunch in the company lounge. Another woman noticed and asked if she could join her. Soon they began quietly discussing what they were reading, and they prayed together. Before long there was a small, but growing, cluster of people informally reading Scripture and talking of their faith each noon hour.

Today, in the company-owned Los Angeles skyscraper, lunch hour gatherings are scheduled three days a week: Bible class on Tuesday, worship service on Wednesday, prayer on Thursday. The corporation allows the group to use available space in the headquarters office without charge. The number who gather in Christ's name often exceeds 150. Other employees often seek out their Christian co-workers as a source of sound advice. And it all began because one woman had the courage to read her Bible openly on her lunch hour.

How about you and me? Does our light shine in our world (Matt. 5:14–16)? Or do we manage to blend into the crowd?

Free to Live!

*D*espite a pressure-cooker life-style, we can avoid the tension and constant, free-floating uneasiness that plague so many. Paul tells us that it's an act of will, a conscious ordering of our thoughts (Phil. 4:4–8). Rather than wait until we "feel" like rejoicing, for example, we *decide* to rejoice ("in the Lord," even if our life at the moment doesn't merit celebration). Contrary to what we often think, emotion follows attitude, not vice versa. We make the choice; then God empowers us to carry out our resolve.

The way we keep all the balls in the air at once, then, is by remembering who we are—and whose we are. It's a continuum:

• My self-identity and sense of self-worth come from knowing that God accepts me as I am, through faith in Jesus Christ.

• Recognizing my dependence on Him, I yield ownership to my life.

• I realize that my abilities and talents are a gift from God, and that I'm to be a faithful steward.

• Because I love Jesus Christ, I want to learn to know Him better; I desire close communication and fellowship with Him. In my Martha-life, I want a Mary-heart (Luke 10:38–42).

That's the integrated life for the Christian working wife— never a victim but rather a victor through Christ's enabling.

I have set before you life and death, blessings and curses. Now choose life, so that you and your children may live and that you may love the Lord your God, listen to his voice, and hold fast to him. —Deut. 30:19–20

It is God who works in you to will and to act according to his good purpose. —Phil. 2:13

2

Count the Cost

I'm a man, but I'm all for women's rights. I never wanted a doormat for a wife. Still, I guess somehow I always thought my wife would be like my mom, after all. You know, baking chocolate-chip cookies and keeping house and . . . being there. But Rosa, she's into her career all the way now, and nothing's the same as it was. I guess it never will be again.
  —Husband

I look at my mother and feel sad for her. Her generation didn't have many alternatives. Yet, in a crazy sort of way, I envy her, too. Mom wistfully points out all my options—and it's true. But maybe those women were the lucky ones.
  —Wife

Chuck still thinks housework is 'woman's work,' so I go home to another full-time job after I finish at the supermarket. I'm perpetually overextended, like a rubber band that's been stretched so often it has lost its spring.
  —Wife

Why does everything else come before me? Like in the evenings, why is it more important for Lori to do her nails and pluck her eyebrows than for us to make love?
  —Husband

For me, freedom would be staying at home with my kids. But that's a luxury we simply can't afford—and neither can most of our friends. Nowadays you can't make it on one income.
    —Wife

Here's the way I see it. Now that we women are allowed to do it all, we're expected to do it all. Please, don't give me any more freedoms—I can't handle any more!
    —Wife

Not so long ago, life was simpler. Males and females knew what was expected of them. They struggled through adolescence, got an education and/or job training, married, and had children. That was simply the way it was, and few thought to question it.

Husbands went off to their jobs, and most wives stayed home. The man was the breadwinner, his job had top priority. The woman typically saw her role as the nurturer. He brought home the paycheck; she gave him emotional support. He provided for their children's physical needs; she took major responsibility for their day-to-day care. He painted the house, mowed the lawn, repaired the car. She cleaned the house, cooked the meals, did the laundry. There was a clear distinction—for most people—between "man's work" and "woman's work."

That line was often crossed, of course. Yet there was a general perception that this was the natural order of affairs. True, the former role perceptions were often stifling and uncreative. For all their drawbacks, however, there was one big plus: they were well defined. By current standards, those life scripts left little opportunity for personal fulfillment. But that same predictability offered security. Boundaries and expectations were clear. Males and females knew when they were—or were not—performing adequately in their roles. They had established standards against which to measure. That's no longer true. Today everything is up for grabs.

A lot of women feel that they've gained something valuable. A lot of men feel that they've lost too much. Many—of both sexes—aren't sure. Inside, they have a vague yearning for a fixed point on the compass of life. Even high achievers (who would never go back in time) often admit to a bit of longing for the old simplicity. As Valerie, a fast-rising young professional puts it, "Aren't there any old-fashioned men around any more? Men who want to marry and settle down? Someone who wants to bring home the bacon to a wife who stays home and fries it?"

Similarly, the older husband who's always been a good provider usually has a difficult time comprehending why his wife would need to seek satisfaction outside their home. Perhaps their children are almost grown or out on their own. Probably he's earning more money than ever before and is ready for more "together time." Why, he wonders, would she now abandon her unscheduled life-style to enter the workaday world? What could she find on the job that she doesn't have at home?

Few younger couples can exercise freedom of choice. The reality of income vs. outgo in many families dictates that both spouses must be gainfully employed. (Women whose salaries go for necessities find it especially distressing that females, on the average, still earn less than their male counterparts—and often for virtually the same work.)

Popular theory has it that most women workers are in white collar jobs, probably because successful women professionals make the news and populate TV programs. But they have uncounted sisters who put in eight hours a day at repetitious, unchallenging factory jobs—or make beds and clean rooms in motels and hotels—or empty bedpans in nursing homes. No glamour here. Just the down-to-earth satisfaction of a paycheck bearing their own names.

T *You're Part of the Majority*

he reasons why women work are as diverse as people themselves. Opinions as to which motivations are "valid" fuel endless discussions. Yet women are holding full-time jobs in ever-increasing numbers. More than one-half the females in the nation are in the work force, and the fastest growing segment is mothers. In fact, the number of work-for-money mothers has quadrupled in the last 30 years.

(All wives and mothers work, of course. That's a given—anywhere, anytime. For brevity's sake, the terms "working wife/mother" and "working couple" on these pages denote individuals who earn a salary for specific tasks, usually outside the home.)

In recent society, most females had it deeply ingrained in them that a woman's happiness was to be found in her marriage, in bearing and nurturing her children, and in furnishing and maintaining a comfortable home. Then the emphasis shifted. The "new-thought experts" announced the end of servility and the beginning of the era of personal independence:

• Don't let people take advantage of you. Demand respect!

• Look out for yourself—first, last, and always!

• Fulfill your potential!

• Get established in your own career; later, perhaps, you might want children—if the timing is right.

• Don't degrade yourself by catering to any man, anywhere.

• You have a right to demand that your husband pleases you!

The result was predictable. Working women in their thirties and over have one foot planted in each world. Many are struggling to be everything that their full-time homemaker mothers were—and also to be as emotionally independent as today's "authorities" advise. When they falter, they remind themselves that down this rocky route lies true happiness.

It seems like a no-win situation. The stay-at-home mother gets the message (spoken or implied) that she's simply vegetating. The working wife/mother, when there are extra demands at her job, feels guilty because she has less time and energy for those she loves. Yet when she must put family over work, she feels that she's shortchanging her job—and perhaps jeopardizing her advancement besides. In either life-style today's woman rarely feels satisfied with her performance. Always the unspoken thought haunts her, "I *should* be doing more."

*T*he recent "me factor" *Is It Worth the Cost? Facing Reality*

*T*he recent "me factor" has complicated life—for housewives as well as employed women. People came to expect unlimited opportunity, unfettered enjoyment of life's never-ending banquet. That seemed not only reasonable and fair but also achievable. After all, hadn't this society been built on each succeeding generation rising higher than its predecessor? We've all heard the story a hundred times. The immigrant, handicapped by poor communication skills and lack of education, nevertheless triumphs because of unyielding will and unflagging effort. Surely we more fortunate individuals could achieve whatever *we* want.

You'll Be Asked to Be Superwoman

So a myth arose, made a place for itself, and settled in to stay: *You can have it all; you can do it all.*

Women greedily gobbled up that theory (though it became our millstone). "Why, of course," we said. "With enough organization, enough determination, we *could* be everything, do everything we wanted to!"

Does that sound too strong? Think about the articles you've read, the "authorities" you've heard on talk shows, the books that make the best-seller list. The style may vary, but the theme seldom deviates. "It's easy," they glibly declare. "All it takes is commitment. Set goals, prioritize, schedule your time. Then you, too, can—and should:

● Be a person who's intellectually growing, physically fit, fun to be around, with a dependably sunny temperament.

- Be a spouse who's always understanding and encouraging, always ready for sex, always positive and interesting. You would never nag—wouldn't dream of complaining!
- Be welded together inseparably with your mate, yet you give each other ample space. You each contribute your all to your marriage and thus meet each other's needs. Romance never fades, because you nourish your relationship—creatively.
- Look younger than you are (forever) and sport a trim, healthy body.
- Dress in style, with a distinctive look that is "you."
- Have a challenging job that is personally satisfying and offers unlimited opportunity for advancement.
- Be an outstanding employee, on your way up the ladder because your employers recognize that you have total commitment and you keep your job skills sharp by continuing education.
- Be an outstanding parent with beautiful, intelligent, well-adjusted, obedient children who never suffer because both parents are employed. You regularly schedule quality time alone with each child.
- Be an active participant in the life of your church.
- Continue growing in your personal faith through regular Bible study and prayer.
- Earn enough money to live the good life.
- Have at least one stimulating hobby.
- Know how to deal with stress and plan for regular recreation—alone, as a couple, as a family.
- Broaden your viewpoint by taking college and/or adult education classes.
- Have a home that's decorated with flair.
- Extend your relaxed hospitality often.
- Have friends and know how to be a friend.
- Keep current with the news and read the latest books.
- Etc.

Take a minute to go through that list again. Check those that have been—or are—your personal goals.

The number of items you've marked probably is staggering. Is it any wonder that you and I walk around tired to the bone, emotionally depleted? Yet when we inevitably stumble, we blame not our overblown expectations but our flawed coping mechanisms. Employed wives/mothers who are financially able to choose other options are especially apt to chide themselves, "You put yourself in this spot, so cut out the complaining and pay the piper."

Reread your list. Anyone can do any of those things—sometimes. Many people can manage part of that list part of the time. But *no one* can be all or do all those things all the time. Each of us has only 24 hours in each day. When we try to pack in what would require 40-hour days and 8-day weeks, we're bound to fail.

Set Your Own Standards

So what do you choose for your own list? What's essential to you? Divide your life into areas (marital relationship, motherhood, job, etc.), rather than try to consider all facets simultaneously. Take time to think each segment through in depth and sort out your personal priorities. That can be difficult, because it calls for hard choices. Try not to be influenced by what your sister, mother, or best friend regard highly. This is, after all, *your* life and marriage.

Don't forget to take into account your individual energy levels. "I learned that the hard way," says Erin. "The gal at the next desk functions very well on five hours of sleep. Every day I'd listen to her detail what she'd been doing, and I'd label myself a failure. I just wasn't trying hard enough! So I started going to bed later and getting up earlier. Kept myself going with black coffee—and sometimes pills. Felt like I was on the ragged edge all the time, but . . . boy, I accomplished a lot! After several months, it all caught up with me. Picked up every 'bug' that came along. The doctor said my resistance was zero and I needed more rest. The lesson was pretty plain: I have to be me."

So accept yourself. Define your desires and goals. Find your own style. Then narrow your perhaps lofty list to what's attainable and/or most urgent. Rank them in order of importance and give those near the top your best effort. Ignore the rest. (It helps to remember that your selections aren't cast in bronze; you can always change your mind.) For if you're to possess mental and emotional well-being, you need to learn to surrender cheerfully what isn't vital for *you*—even though it may take precedence for others.

And be patient. Later, you'll probably be able to pursue some interests and activities you must shut the door on for now. If you're self-disciplined enough to limit your involvements, you'll reap the benefits: uncommitted time and space to assuage your constant time pressure, enhanced enjoyment of what you *do* undertake.

Today growing numbers of women—and men—are recognizing anew the wisdom of accommodating life as it is, rather than of dreaming dreams that are clearly impossible and therefore frustrating. So the pendulum is beginning to swing back to center. Encouraging indications are that we're entering a period of more reality. A few of the current crop of experts are saying, "It's ridiculous to try to be Superwoman. You can't do it all—and you shouldn't even try."

One of these days, you and I might believe them!

Your Christianity Will Be Challenged

The Bible essentially is silent on working couples, except for a few examples. Priscilla worked with her husband, Aquila, as a tentmaker (Acts 18:2–3). The "virtuous woman" of Prov. 31:10–28 (often held up to Christian women as a role model of the good wife) obviously did not stay home as a full-time homemaker. She supervised servants, bought land and paid for it, had a separate income, planted a vineyard, carried on profitable trade, aided the poor, and supplied merchants with sashes, presumably to be sold. Her intelligence, enterprise, and dignity brought honor to her husband. Lydia (Acts 16::14–15), a woman of means, dealt in expensive purple cloth. So there were "working wives" in the Bible.

In spite of that, Christian dual-career couples often are dismayed to find that family, friends, or fellow church members disapprove of their life-style. The criticism may be either open or subtle, but it hurts, and it compounds any guilt with which the couple already struggles.

Blame for the disastrous rise in divorces and the breakdown of family life is often laid at the feet of the working wife. Critics predict lifetime harm to children in such homes. These opinions remain opinions, however. The jury is still out on whether children will grow up more self-reliant or lastingly insecure. It's simply too soon to know.

Traditional marriages—with stay-at-home wives—may be held up as examples of "the more excellent way." Surely, no one should put down the wife/mother who devotes herself to her family. (Indeed, that life-style gets little affirmation from society, even though there's no work as important as raising God-fearing, secure children.) Yet it's interesting, isn't it, that hardly anyone criticizes the full-time homemaker/mother who is up to her armpits in volunteerism and classes of one kind or another. She may be out of the home more than her employed counterpart!

Consider two typical married women. Here's one week's schedule of Sharon Smith, full-time homemaker:

Monday
  Morning: Aerobics
  Afternoon: Help produce Christian braille books
  Evening: Church Board of Education meeting

Tuesday
  Morning: Weekly women's Bible class at church
  Afternoon: Deliver Meals on Wheels; art lesson
  Evening: Craft group working on items for the church
    bazaar

Wednesday
    Morning: Aerobics; photography class
    Afternoon: Library volunteer
    Evening: Choir practice

Thursday
    Morning: Volunteer work at hospital gift shop
    Afternoon: Deliver Meals on Wheels; grocery shopping and
        running errands for senior citizens
    Evening: Sunday school teachers meeting

Friday
    Morning: Aerobics
    Afternoon: Volunteer in church office
    Evening: Small-group Bible study with husband

Saturday
    Morning: Altar Guild
    Afternoon: Volunteer at local historical site open on week-
        ends
    Evening: *Free, at home*

Sunday
    Morning: Sing solo in early worship service; teach Sunday
        school; sing with choir in 11:00 service
    Afternoon: Provide music twice a month for worship ser-
        vices at local nursing home
    Evening: *Free, at home*

Betty Brown, on the other hand, has this weekly schedule:

Monday through Friday
    Morning and Afternoon: Employed 8:00 a.m. to 5:00 p.m.
    Evenings: *Free, at home*, except for Friday's small group
Bible study with husband

Saturday: *Free, at home*

Sunday
    Morning: Attend church and Sunday school as a family
    Afternoon and Evening: *Free, at home*

Women such as Sharon Smith usually are sincerely committed to serving others and definitely fill many needs. Fellow Christians praise them loud and long:

"She's such a good worker!"

"You can always count on Sharon."

"Don't know how we'd keep the church going without her!"

It's all true—and laudable. However, the Sharons are not necessarily "full-time" homemakers—at least, not in terms of the number of hours.

Nevertheless, the Bettys get bad press.

"She works, you know, so she's not very involved in the church. That's what always happens when a woman takes a job. I guess it's up to the rest of us to pick up the slack."

"Must be hard on her family, her being gone all day like that. I wouldn't want *my* kids to spend so much time alone!"

A word to the wise: Consider the source of such criticism and be prepared. Be aware that critics may be (a) seeking to justify their own life choices; (b) trying to resolve their feelings, pro and con; (c) gathering firsthand background information before making a change in their own lives; or (d) sincerely concerned for your welfare and your marriage (although what's meant to be affection may feel like a reproach.)

Occasionally you may feel singled out by your pastor's sermon topic or by casual remarks in a Bible class. Is your attitude, by any chance, defensive or apologetic? If so, you're likely to pick up such messages, whether or not they're being sent.

Resolve not to take such comments as a personal attack. Remember, no one else has the power to make you angry or to fill you with guilt. You choose your own emotions.

Decide for yourself how you'll handle criticism. Ignore the remarks and they'll fade away. Or agree with the speaker and then change the subject. ("Yes, I suppose there may be some truth in what you say, but it seems to be working well for us. By the way, wasn't that an interesting speaker?") With some people it's worth the effort to talk through the issue calmly and openly. If you've thought through your responses beforehand

and have a balanced approach, the disapproval will diffuse itself.

It's not necessary to defend your life-style or to dazzle critics with caustic comebacks. All that's necessary to remain unruffled is that *you* know your reasons and are convinced of their validity.

Rather than turning away, hurt and angry, turn *toward* those who differ. (That's hardly a natural reaction.) Let them get to know you as an individual. Allow them to discover that your marriage and family life are not only intact but alive, strong, and solid. As an employed couple living out your lives and interacting within your circle of friends and acquaintances, you can demonstrate your continuing commitment to God and each other. In that way you'll be the best advertisement for the strength of the two-paycheck Christian marriage and family.

Translating Your Stated Salary into Net Income

"Well, you can always quit if you're fed up," a husband may say to his employed wife. But it's not quite that simple—and they both know it. Her income provides definite benefits. However, their *net* gain may be less than they suppose. Most people compute the obvious costs—commuting expenses, parking fees, lunches, expanded wardrobe, union dues, and child care.

Remember to include also costs that aren't so apparent. For instance, the added income likely pushes you into a higher tax bracket, both federal and state. The typical working wardrobe is likely to require dry cleaning rather than being wash-and-wear. If you drive your own car, wear will accelerate as mileage adds up faster. Remember, too, that food costs are almost inevitably higher for the two-income couple. When both spouses are tired at the end of the day, a fast-food meal and no dishes look mighty attractive. So do prepared dinners from the frozen-foods case.

Children left in day-care centers or group care are statistically more likely to pick up colds and respiratory infections, as well as other illnesses, so medical costs may increase. Add in also the cost of providing alternative child care or taking off work yourself when a sick child must stay at home.

This isn't to imply that if your net income is less than you anticipated, you have no business being employed. Just be aware of the facts. Recognize that working not only pays, it also costs. So get a fix on the dollars-and-cents price of having a job.

Your Family Time Will Be Reduced

As a working woman, you may be disquieted by nebulous feelings of guilt. Perhaps you feel that your life is a constant balancing act between your career and your family. You may judge that somehow you're cheating your children, even though you're convinced that you have no other choice.

Wherever you are right now, it's vital to shut the door on past failures and deficiencies and *start where you are.*

Examine your situation. Make carefully considered choices—and then "murder the alternatives." Try to assess objectively your options, your preferences, your needs. Seek out a competent professional counselor if you feel that you "can't see the forest for the trees." But cut out—forever—the self-blame, the "if onlys," the accusations. Refuse to look back with longing on what might have been. Perpetual second-guessing leaves you emotionally exhausted and elevates tension levels while accomplishing nothing.

Still, be realistic. Count also the nonfinancial costs: added time pressure, emotional struggle as you ponder the effects of day care, the double responsibility of filling two roles. Are they too costly? Will they hurt your marriage? your children? No one but you can make that decision. In every life-style, some families turn out well-balanced children—and some don't.

The point is, make your own choices; don't just follow the crowd—any crowd. Know *your* reasons. Decide on *your* goals, together, as wife and husband. Ask the Lord for guidance, too. You don't know all the answers and can't see the final effects of your actions. But He does. Use your God-given reason, enlightened by the Holy Spirit. Then exercise your best judgment to arrive at a course of action—and be willing to pay the price.

Is There a Way to Cut the Cost?

While the above assumes a full-time position, you may have alternatives you haven't considered. If your present employment entails lots of overtime and is extremely demanding, you may be able to find a comparable position in another company where the pace is slower.

Consider another option that often works well: job sharing (two people sharing the same full-time position). Sometimes there's an equal division of hours; in other cases, one individual works two full workdays and the other three. Half the salary of a full-time position may be more than the hourly wage paid part-time workers. Perhaps you could identify another person with similar skills—and with whom you feel compatible—and apply together to share the same job position. That person might be your spouse. For example, two teachers, married to each other, may share the same teaching position so that one parent or the other can always be with their children.

For some, a part-time rather than a full-time job may appear to be the best answer. But a part-time job sometimes carries disproportionate costs. You'll still need suitable clothing and must find responsible child care. If you work five half-days, commuting expense will be the same as for full-time employment (unless you pay for parking by the hour). You probably won't receive any fringe benefits such as hospitalization insurance, dental plan, savings plan, etc. (That may not matter if you're covered under your spouse's plan.) Often, too, you'll be paid an hourly wage instead of a salary—and most of the time that's lower than for the same job, full-time. Nevertheless, in survey after survey, mothers of young children state that they prefer part-time work. One young mother put her reasons this way:

"I didn't want to look back one day and realize that I'd missed most of my daughter's early years. With a full-time job, I'd probably miss most of Kelly's 'firsts'—the first step, the first word. At least my chances of being there are better with a part-time job. And if all that research about the importance of the first five years is true, this is when she'll be formulating her outlook on life. I want her values to come from my husband and me, not someone else—even if that person is reliable and well-intentioned."

As a third option, consider flex-time, where workers set their own schedules. It's usually a hit with employees, and it's a growing trend. There are several methods. For instance, within specified hours workers may come and go on their own timetable. Some businesses even allow that option during the entire 24 hours. In other businesses, workers can choose to work four 10-hour days—leaving them a three-day weekend every week.

Your employer, like most, may not make either flex-time or job sharing available. Most are reluctant to depart from well-established business practice and to chance an experiment. But the support of fellow workers and a well-researched proposal may be all it takes to effect a change by management.

As a fourth possibility, some women consider becoming an Office Temporary, in their view, the best of both worlds. When there's a special family event or simply extra-heavy demands—when a child is ill, when they have the opportunity to accompany their husband on a business trip—the Office Temp is free to say, "I don't want to work that day/week." By contrast, other women consider being a Temp a dead end. Temporary workers may/do miss out on possible advancement, unless they choose to accept a full-time position. However, many temporary employment firms now offer their own group health insurance and other benefits.

Don't overlook the possibility of working at home, either. There are growing numbers of entrepreneurs who've success-fully escaped the structured 9-to-5 world. You're limited only by your creativity. Here are just a few options, workable no matter where you live:

Catering service
Bookkeeping service

Computer programming or word processing at home by contract

Transcribing legal or medical records

Typing for others (e.g., college theses, resumes, reports, etc.)

Putting on birthday parties (some even provide pony rides, do magic acts, or train their pets to perform)

Tutoring

Chauffeuring children to after-school lessons/activities

Running errands for others

House-sitting

Unpacking service for people who've moved

Addressing Christmas and birthday cards for a fee

Personal shopping; wardrobe advice/shopping; gift shopping

Interior decorating advice/coordination

House-cleaning services

Etc.

The big advantage to working out of your own home goes beyond the financial. You'll have more flexibility. You can spend more time with your children—often even taking them along. And you'll have the satisfaction of using your own creative effort and seeing the direct reward. The key is to search out the need(s) in your area that aren't already being met adequately.

A Whatever the Cost, You Can Make It Work

All marriages are alike, yet each is unique. No one can lay down rigid theories for success, because the two persons in any marriage are always one-of-a-kind. Yet there are valid areas of comparison, principles that build closeness and strength between you.

1. Know that reinforcing your union is essential. Added time pressure, fatigue, and the stress of trying to hold it all together wear away at your relationship. After all, it takes energy to contribute to a marriage. And like that of every other mortal, your vitality is limited.

2. For any married couple, but especially for the two-career couple, it's crucial to be of one mind. In every situation, aim to overlook your differences and to concentrate on your sense of oneness. Resolve to ignore whatever would tear at your marriage bond. Your most important asset is the feeling that you're both committed—that you're a team with a shared purpose. Hammer out your mutual objective—together—and be sure each clearly perceives it. If one flounders at times, the partner can lovingly remind the other where you're aiming. As the prophet Amos admonished the children of Israel centuries ago, "Can two walk together, except they be agreed?" (Amos 3:3 KJV)

3. In the happiest pairings, each is the other's best friend. If you're a working couple with a sense of partnership that supersedes preoccupation with your jobs, you'll reap unexpected dividends. You'll have the joy of knowing that it's okay not to be completely self-sufficient—and to admit it. You can lean on each other, draw support from each other, and not feel any loss of self-esteem. Indeed, you both will realize that interdependence is a major source of strength.

4. It's comforting to note that when divorces occur, they occur because of any number of basic deficiencies in a couple's relationship. The blame can't be laid solely on the wife's employment. (That, however, may be a catalyst when there are other difficulties.) You can maintain a solid relationship—with mutual effort, as always—whether your marriage is composed of one or two wage-earning partners.

5. Striving toward shared goals, focusing on your oneness, discussing your feelings openly—these are the essentials. Your unity in Jesus Christ as Savior and Lord of your life, of your marriage and family, is your foundation and strength. The harmony evident in your union will bear this out.

The times we live in are not easy. What used to be fixed and predictable is now always in flux.People switch jobs many times in their lives. Hardly anyone goes to work for the XYZ Company expecting to stay long enough to collect a gold watch at retirement.

Patterns within marriage, too, are subject to outward change. That means that husbands and wives can expect to keep on adjusting throughout their life together. But that's no cause for apprehension. The qualities that make a marriage work in every circumstance are mutual love and commitment to the union and faith in God, which undergirds the couple every step of the way. That will carry marriage partners through anything—not always smoothly, perhaps, but strongly.

Make no mistake about it. The two-income marriage, simply put, is a continuing challenge, even when both spouses are emotionally stable and have wholehearted determination. The rewards can be great and varied, but it's never a free ride.

No one is happy or free who lives only for himself. Joy in living comes from immersion in something one recognizes to be bigger, better, worthier, and more enduring than he himself is. True happiness and true freedom come from squandering one's self for a purpose. (Carl W. McGeehon)

In marriage, being the right person is as important as finding the right person. (Wilbert Donald Gough)

Marriages are made in heaven, but they are lived on earth. (George P. Weiss)

3

Growing as Christian Marriage Partners

The woman was formed out of man—not out of his head to rule over him; not out of his feet to be trod upon by him; but out of his side to be his equal, from beneath his arm to be protected, and from near his heart to be loved.
 —*Matthew Henry*

To truly respect one another, you need to respect yourself first. A lot of the competition within marriage comes from one or both partners having a low self-image. Two healthy persons each make up one-half of a healthy relationship.
 —*Wife*

Marriage—a community consisting of a master, a mistress, and two slaves—making in all, two.
 —*Ambrose Bierce*

When people are serving, life is no longer meaningless.
 —*John Gardner*

Two individuals. Two halves of the same whole. Two people who draw their sense of values and self-worth not from outside circumstances but from within. Two people, each with a strong personal identity.

We live in an era when personal identity and freedom are much talked about. Both qualities are considered essential for wholeness. Yet how do we reconcile that concept with marriage as a *union* of two persons, two lives into one? If we're to make marriage work, we are told, "we" must become more important than "I" and "me." The Bible says virtually the same thing: "For this reason a man will leave his father and mother and be united to his wife, and they will become one flesh" (Gen. 2:24).

"One flesh," however, doesn't mean being fused so that the two individuals become indistinguishable. Instead, each person is one-half of a couple. The marriage relationship can only be as sound and strong and secure as the two people in it and what each brings to their life together.

T *My Identity as a Child of God*

he way to start discovering the strength of our union is to discern who we are, what makes us what we are, and what we want to become. Those factors determine how we relate to others as well as how we'll cope with life's demands. It requires no flashes of brilliance to ascertain that the dual-career couple's life is composed of a succession of strenuous days. That mandates a strong self-image and a clear set of values within each one. We need to know not only what we're doing but why.

Think about it. What's the source of our self-worth and our identity? What makes me, me, and you, you? Is it our work? Whether or not we have children? Our ethnic roots? Our income level? The clothes we wear and/or the car we drive? Whether we're well respected and liked by our peers or on the outer fringes of the "in" group? Or is that self-image meant to proceed from within us, untainted by outside influences and situations?

As Christians we needn't go far to find the answer. God,

through the writers of Scripture, often describes our position as "in Christ." We needn't work toward that relationship or qualify in any way. It is settled—a pure gift that comes when we know Jesus Christ as our Savior from sin (John 5:24; Rom. 8:14–16; 1 Peter 2:9–10). Our self-confidence proceeds out of our inner security in Christ.

If we flounder, the cause can't be traced to any alteration in our identity as God's beloved children, because that does not vary. People around us may be mired in uncertainty and self-reproach. But as Christians we can shed the constricting garment of self-doubt and condemnation and uncertainty—if we take God at His word.

The term "identity crisis" has been in fashion for quite some time and has become a catchphrase, carelessly tossed about. Most of us possess at least a hazy understanding of its meaning. (Some of us have lived through that unnerving ordeal without having a handy label.) In brief, there's a feeling of turmoil, sometimes of being shaken to your roots.

One person who was anguishing through the experience tried to explain:

"I don't really understand what's wrong with me. I'm doing now what I've always done—and I thought I had a good life. Yet now I'm unsure, somehow, about everything. It's like having all the props knocked out from under me—by what or whom, I don't know—and endlessly floundering, unable to get a solid footing. I don't like myself much right now. I thought I was stronger than this."

Perhaps this condition is as old as mankind and we've just bestowed a name. Or perhaps the phenomenon spread because of the multiplicity of options available to us.

Putting First Things First

That endless smorgasbord of opportunities makes it harder to choose. Saying "yes" to one thing means saying "no" to a host of others. And which takes precedence?

As Suzanne puts it, "Am I a wife first or a mother first? Or am I an employee first, because my hours are fixed and I'm being paid for my time? When my first-grader has a runny nose and a 100° temperature, do I send him to school because my boss is depending on me? Or do I call in sick and lie, because if I miss too many days off, I'll lose my job? Then we couldn't afford to send my son and daughter to a Christian school. And in our neighborhood, the public school is really bad—poor teachers and a big drug problem.

"So tell me—please, somebody, tell me!" continues Suzanne. "What is the *right* thing to do? Whom do I put first? How do I even figure out what *is* first?"

The quandary is universal. Even Christians sometimes struggle to make sense out of their lives. Feelings of frustration and emptiness aren't a recent discovery, as the writer of Ecclesiastes movingly expresses:

> When I surveyed all that my
>   hands had done
>   and what I had toiled to achieve,
> everything was meaningless,
>   a chasing after the wind;
>   nothing was gained under the sun.
>
> (Eccl. 2:11)

Those words could have been written today, couldn't they? They express the emptiness so many feel in spite of personal achievement and the trappings of success.

So how do you and I live out our lives now, in these times? We do it the way people always have, whether or not they admitted it. We make our decisions based on our individual values, open or unexpressed. As Christians, our foundation for everything else is that we're children of God—redeemed sinners and heirs of heaven.

Sorting Out Our Obligations

In personal relationships, the wife's first obligation is to be the wife Christ would have us be. Since Scripture expressly states that children are God's gift to us (Ps. 113:9; 127:3), they are our second responsibility—and privilege (Deut. 6:6–9; Ps. 78:4–7; Prov. 22:6; Joel 1:3). As for our work, when we accept a job, we're entering into a contract to use our abilities whole-heartedly in return for our wages.

Within our personal style and talents, these become the measure by which we gauge alternatives and make choices:

1. My Savior has a right to a follower who's growing in faith and discipleship through personal Bible study and prayer and through faithful, regular worship with fellow believers.

2. My husband has a right to a wife who's committed, available, interested, supportive, and loving.

3. My children have a right to a mother who gives them love, attention, and care; who imparts the Christian faith and principles by word and example; who is simply there when they want/need me.

4. My employer has a right to expect me to put forth a day's work for a day's pay—to be loyal and honest.

Though this sounds formidable at first reading, in day-to-day living the balance will shift. For example, when I spend every night of the week sewing a costume for my daughter's play, she's (temporarily) taking first place. When the fiscal year ends at work, and I must work overtime for a few weeks, my husband and family will necessarily see much less of me.

You and I, of course, make the same adaptations when our husbands are pressed. These are normal aspects of family living. We may feel a bit neglected, but we recognize that love hasn't died. We have a time problem, not a relationship problem.

The writer of Ecclesiastes reminds us how we're enabled to cope with these inevitable ups and downs of life: "A cord of three strands is not quickly broken" (4:12). In the Christian marriage, those "three strands" are God, the husband, and the wife. For when God is a real part of our life together—and of our individual walk—we have His strength to draw on. His enabling power will ease us through the tough times and hold us as one. The majesty of His promises runs throughout the

Bible—for example, Ps. 34:15, 17; 145:18–19; John 16:23–27; Heb. 10:22–23.

Despite such solid reassurance, most of us experience occasional lapses of confidence about our life choices. It helps to remember that everyone else does, too. No one's life is perfect, even though our hindsight may be. Yet we do have the guarantee that God will turn everything to our good (Rom. 8:28), even our mistakes and failures. So when you face a new outbreak of uncertainty, whether about the future or the past, don't endlessly play that broken record in your mind. Learn to give your load to God before you waste time and energy mulling it over. Be open to the Lord's leading. If you're on the wrong track, He'll show you. If you've prayed for guidance and don't feel led to make changes, relax. Doubts remain part of the human condition.

Make It a Duet

As your husband shares the details of his workday with you, make a mental note of his concerns and pray for him. If he's a Christian, ask him to pray for you. Even better, pray *with* him. We often long for a prayer partner—someone with whom we can share our deepest thoughts, someone who cares and will support us, emotionally as well as by lifting our requests before the Lord. What better "two" than the two of you (Matt. 18:20)?

Some couples hold hands and both pray silently; others take turns. Or if one partner feels ill at ease, the spouse most comfortable praying aloud may lead while the other prays along silently. (If you feel awkward at first, you're normal.)

"Joel and I were married for 20 years before we got up the courage to pray together," says Rita. "Can you believe that? I thought we'd covered every topic under the sun, yet we were as tongue-tied as strangers. So we just hung in there until we got over our stage fright. Our prayer time has become very precious—I think we really do share our inner selves now as never before. I can't tell you how it touches my heart when Joel thanks God for me!"

48

If you're spiritually single, you likely ache for your husband to walk with the Lord. Pour out that unique loneliness to the Lord and He will comfort you. Remember that how you relate as a wife, a mother, and a neighbor bears powerful witness (1 Peter 3:1–2). Your loving attitude will be far more effective than frequently telling your husband how much he needs Christ in his life. As one woman put it, "Don't talk to your husband about God; talk to God about your husband." Commit your partner to the Lord, and trust His Holy Spirit to lead him to faith in Jesus Christ.

When your spirit lags, draw fresh strength from recalling that God will—in His time—use the day-to-day evidence of your life. As surely as a magnet attracts steel, your husband will be influenced toward the Savior by your sincere, godly demeanor. And if you don't see any change, don't feel guilty. Bringing your husband to faith is the Holy Spirit's responsibility. Yours is simply to witness.

As Children of God, Who's in Charge?

The controversy continues. The Biblical concept of headship and submission often seems a tired, tattered remnant from long ago, especially to the working wife who brings in a respectable share of the family income. She may also bear major responsibility for home management and for child care. Pushed to the limit at times, she's justly proud of her initiative and independence.

Current societal thinking describes marriage as an equal partnership. "There's no place for dominance, no problem that good communication can't solve," we're told. Besides, today's crop of experts agrees that we humans are happiest when we're assertive, self-sufficient, self-actualizing; when we set goals and then go for them; when we not only dream but savor the satisfaction of achieving on our own; when we enlightened women rightly demand fair treatment and respect in the workplace and at home; when we expect that our spouses will share responsibilities in the home.

Such thinking permeates our minds and colors our attitudes, however subtly. Men as well as women often question (if not flatly reject) the Scriptural teaching that wives are to be subject, obedient(!) to their husbands. Many feel, "I thought we'd left that archaic notion behind."

And so we could—except for one "minor" detail: the Bible is all of a piece. Our knowledge of redemption through Christ is based on the unchanging words of God, inspired through His Holy Spirit (John 20:31; 2 Peter 1:21). So when we accept the Gospel as valid, we accept the rest of Scripture along with it. Try as we might, we can't escape it: God's basic pattern for marriage remains today as it did 2,000 years ago. God names the husband as head of the house, whether or not the husband exercises that position or even qualifies for it.

"I guess that hits me right in the pride," says Jackie. "I don't know of anything in this world that's harder for me than the idea of submitting—to anyone! Why should Darrell get to call the shots for both of us?"

How do you react? Do you applaud this relationship style as "the only one which works"? Do you judge this to be a demeaning attitude toward females, set forth by an unmarried (male) apostle, and ignore it? Do you prefer to develop your own balance, drawing on the latest and best knowledge from psychology and human relations advisors? Perhaps you believe the Bible, yet feel that parts of it can't possibly apply to modern times.

"I've gone to Bible classes faithfully for years," says Adele. "But sometimes Scripture seems, well, kind of irrelevant—especially compared to the writers and doctors and the authorities I see on TV talk shows. I mean, those people have done all kinds of research, using the latest techniques. Somehow, they make more sense. I can identify with them, you know? They're alive and breathing and talking, you know? They have the facts on what people are like nowadays. And God, well, to begin with, He's invisible and remote and . . . "

Perhaps Adele speaks for you. True, books and speakers and psychological studies are often helpful. Yet if we're wise, we'll evaluate every theory, every opinion—carefully, thought-fully, and prayerfully. Our plumb line is God's revealed Word and the witness of our own spirits as His children. Then we'll have a time-tested, solid basis on which to build our lives (Rom. 1:16–17; 8:5–11; 12:1–2; 15:4).

Why? It's My Life, Isn't It?

More than ever before, we women pride ourselves on our independence. So submission, even if it once seemed somewhat appropriate, has become a red-flag word. We judge that husbands and wives are the haves and the have-nots, the powerful and the powerless. As so often happens, we humans have missed God's original meaning. God's point is not who wields the power but rather who's responsible for what.

Strange, isn't it? No one questions the fact that a business needs someone in charge. In fact, if we compare the operating style of a business or an office to that of a marriage, we may be able to examine this issue more objectively.

For instance, in business the manager and staff have different areas in which they exercise authority. The manager directs the employees, but the owner or the board of directors holds him accountable for the success or failure of the operation. The wise administrator treats personnel with consideration, tact, and kindness. Such a supervisor becomes the employees' encourager and supporter as well as their director. These managers are respected not because they demand it but because they earn it.

Savvy supervisors realize that from the top level down to the lowest-paid employee, each person is essential to maintaining the business. Each works for the common good toward a mutual goal. Employees, on the other hand, recognize that they function best when someone "sees the big picture" and sets policy. When opinions between staff members and/or departments differ, the manager hears the evidence, then makes the final decision. Each person involved is equally important, but their responsibilities differ.

Similarly, God doesn't intend that husbands are to rule as dictators. Rather, the Bible cites God's Son as our example. Jesus submitted willingly to His Father (Luke 22:42; John 12:27–28). On occasion, Christ even volunteered for the work of the lowest slave, admonishing His disciples to do likewise (Luke 22:24–27; John 13:13–17). Jesus was modeling behavior both for the Twelve and for you and me—as His follower and as a spouse (Phil. 2:1–11). The pattern is the same. As individual Christians, first we submit to the Lord and then to each other—*as unto Christ*.

There's no hint here as to who *gives* orders and who *takes* them. Nor is the issue who manages the money and who cleans the house. We're free to work out those details according to individual talents and preferences.

Nevertheless, along with that freedom of choice come some definite principles. Let's look at the husband's role first. (Since one English word seldom includes all the nuances of the original Greek, several Bible translations are quoted.) St. Paul's very first sentence of this discourse on submission/headship sets the stage:

> Be subject to one another out of reverence for Christ. (Eph. 5:21 NEB)

Husband and wife are to be *mutually* submissive. Each wants the welfare of the other. Each respects and nurtures the other.

> The man is the head of the woman, just as Christ also is the head of the church. . . . Husbands, love your wives, as Christ also loved the church and gave himself up for it. . . . In the same way men also are bound to love their wives, as they love their own bodies. In loving his wife a man loves himself. For no one ever hated his own body: on the contrary, he provides and cares for it; and that is how Christ treats the church, because it is his body, of which we are living parts. Thus it is that (in the words of Scripture) 'a man shall leave his father and mother and shall be joined to his wife, and

the two shall become one flesh.' . . . each of you must love his wife as his very self." (Eph. 5:23, 25, 28–31 NEB)

Paul makes a similar point in Col. 3:19:

Husbands, love your wives and do not be harsh with them. (NIV)

Peter stresses the same theme in 1 Peter 3:7:

Likewise you husbands, live considerately with your wives, bestowing honor on the woman. (RSV)

Or as stated in the NIV:

. . . treat them with respect.

The husband is to consider his wife's feelings as important as his own. He's to exhibit empathy, love, and sympathy; to be consistently kind and compassionate; to set no limits on his acceptance and/or forgiveness. It wouldn't occur to this husband that his wife is his servant or his inferior. Nor would he dream of asking her to compromise her personal principles. He *respects* her.

But wait! There's more—this from the apostle Paul in Eph. 6:4:

Do not exasperate your children. (NIV)

Or as Phillips paraphrases:

Fathers, don't over-correct your children or make it difficult for them to obey the commandment. Bring them up with Christian teaching in Christian discipline.

Paul emphasizes much the same point in Col. 3:21:

Fathers, do not embitter your children, or they will become discouraged. (NIV)

Fathers are to be actively involved in training and disciplining their children—remembering that children are children. They're to tailor discipline to the child's age and spirit, always with gentleness. They're to exercise restraint, so that their offspring don't become resentful.

So you see, Paul has hardly given the husband—as some argue—a kingly position with all the perks of royalty. Instead, as Harry Truman said, "The buck stops here!" In God's arrangement, it is the *man* who is finally accountable to God for the state of affairs within the marriage and family. As Christ was, so he's to be a *servant*-leader (John 13:12–17).

Help Your Husband Develop

"My husband's a great guy, but he mostly does *his* thing," exclaims Janice, " . . . his job, his Saturday golf game with the guys, his woodworking out in the garage, his TV shows. He never mistreats any of us . . . never gives orders. He's just uninvolved. In fact, I pretty much run this family single-handedly. Somebody has to."

"That's the way Ben used to be, too," says Natalie. "But one day, when I complained to my wise old neighbor, she said, 'My dear, a man will only assume as much authority as a woman will *allow* him. If you step back a foot or two and *let* Ben take charge, he will.'

"So I decided to try it," Natalie continues. "What did I have to lose? I started with our paychecks. I've always managed our money because I'm better with numbers. But Ben never stuck to his allowance. He has a mania for gadgets of all kinds and was forever bringing home something he'd put on our charge cards. Made me so mad! Naturally, we'd have a big fight. He'd either keep it, which made me furious, or take it back, which he said made him feel like a naughty kid. Actually, I did feel like his mother—or his keeper.

"So when I announced that from then on he was in charge of the money, neither one of us could believe it. Keeping my mouth shut almost choked me! That first year he paid most bills late, so we had extra finance charges. The telephone company even shut off the phone one month. But slowly Ben began to change in many ways. He became stronger somehow. I liked that!

"Next I asked him to help the kids with their Sunday school memory work, and that went okay. Later he took over car-pool duty to get them to Wednesday church school. Some Saturdays he suggested skipping golf and took the kids hiking instead. Those Saturday outings got to be a habit. When the kids had problems, I stopped handling them alone. Once I'd had all the answers. Now I deliberately asked Ben, 'What do *you* think?' And I found he was listening, really listening. He cared!

"I was afraid that he'd be turned off by all the responsibility," Natalie continues. "But the funny thing is that the more he took charge, the more interested and involved he became. For instance, the other day he called me from work because he'd been thinking about Jared's low math grades and how we could help him. The old Ben would never have done that— wouldn't even have noticed!

"I wouldn't say it has been easy," says Natalie, "but it's been worth it. I guess Ben couldn't be the head of the house as long as *I* was. And honestly, I haven't lost any rights. Probably gained some. I used to think Ben and I were sparring partners, and we still fight sometimes. But there's more comfort, more love between us now. I feel cherished. Funny how something labeled 'submission' could make me feel freer than ever before."

A Word to the Wives

Natalie's experience is a good illustration of Paul's plain word for you and me paraphrased gently by Phillips:

> And "fit in with" each other, because of your common reverence for Christ. You wives must learn to adapt yourselves to your husbands, as you submit yourselves to the Lord, for the husband is the "head" of the wife in the same way that Christ is head of the Church and savior of the Body. The willing subjection of the Church to Christ should be reproduced in the submission of wives to their husbands. . . . let every wife respect her husband. (Eph. 5:21–24, 33)

The NIV concludes that section with "the wife must respect her husband." Note Paul's context: "as you submit yourselves to the Lord."

"Adapt" . . . "respect" . . . "fit in with" . . . "submit"—not words we modern daughters of Eve want to hear. Clearly, God appointed the husband to be in charge and the wife to yield—whether that pleases us or not. We who matter-of-factly accept direction on the job often find it distasteful in our homes.

Think about the typical hassles of a typical married couple. John has an exciting job offer on the other side of the country; Mary wants to stay where she is. John wants to leave their mutually acquired savings in nice, safe municipal bonds; Mary wants to invest a sizable chunk to open a small business of her own. Mary would like to consolidate their vacation time and set off on a trip to Europe; John would rather have several short vacations and stay in this country. John wants his widowed mother to move in with them; Mary is uncomfortable with that prospect.

This hypothetical couple has gathered facts and listed priorities—listed everything, in fact. They've argued their individual points endlessly, but neither has swayed the other. Obviously, they can't both move and stay, can't save their money and spend it. Unless they want to be deadlocked forever—or continue to vacillate—*someone* must make a decision.

But there's the rub. When you and I find ourselves in an either/or situation, we find it extremely hard to say, "You decide, Dear," even though we know that our husband loves us and wants our best. Are we afraid that today he makes one decision and tomorrow he takes over _all_ of them? Or could it be that we simply want that power ourselves?

Don't think that "submissive" is meant to be synonymous with "doormat." Nor are healthy self-esteem and a desire to achieve either wrong or sinful. Consider again the "wife of noble character":

> Her husband has full confidence in her
>   and lacks nothing of value.
> She brings him good, not harm,
>   all the days of her life. . . .
> Her husband is respected at the city gate,

where he takes his seat
among the elders of the land.
(Prov. 31:11–12, 23)

Earlier verses reveal that this talented, capable working wife has authority in many areas. Since she successfully pursues many activities, she must feel pleased with herself and with what she accomplishes—and she should! Yet the verses above plainly signal that the husband is head of the household.

Today, too, the employed wife may exercise far-reaching control in her job. She may supervise a group of men and women,manage large sums of money, or head a thriving corporation. Nevertheless, whether she has spent the day designing an ad campaign for a Fortune 500 company or has stood on her feet taking orders at a hamburger stand, when she leaves the workplace, those New Testament verses say that she's to be submissive in her marriage relationship. That's not an easy transition!

And it baffles the modern mind. Put simply, *why* would an all-knowing God still ask that same mind-set from today's wives? Why should a standard imposed many centuries ago still apply to women who are fully competent to earn their own living and to manage their own lives?

We may not know God's reason, but this we know for sure: Our loving Creator ordained that position for you and me—for His reasons—for our good.

For Women Only

If this arrangement rankles, remember also that God, in His unfathomable wisdom, bestowed the privilege of birthing children to women alone. How many of us would choose to relinquish our right to bear children? Yet that privilege costs us dearly. Nine months of pregnancy can be nine months of discomfort. Giving birth is filled with searing pain. And being a mother day by day is no pushover. Personal time and self-indulgence become more wish than reality as we yield ourselves and our prerogatives to serve. Our reward? The joy of that unique bond between mother and child, the feeling of accomplishment as we watch our children mature, the satisfaction of sacrifice—in love.

Just as motherhood is a *continuing* challenge, so is allowing our husbands to exercise their right of headship. Not only are we unenthusiastic, but the very idea raises our hackles. What gets in the way carries an ugly name: Pride. (We'd probably consider this a marvelous arrangement if the roles were reversed.)

As always, it comes back to attitude. If we consider submission to be bondage, it will be. (Similarly, motherhood can either be regarded as 20 years of slavery and sacrifice or as two decades spent nurturing and shaping human beings.) If we concentrate on restrictions, real and imagined, we'll feel caged. Or we can resolve that our relationship with our husbands shall be an opportunity to demonstrate our devotion to *Christ* in a practical way. Then submission takes on a different nature. Yielding then becomes our freely given gift, laid at the feet of Jesus through yielding to our husbands. It doesn't even matter whether our husband "deserves" our respect. The key lies in keeping our eyes on Christ. Somehow, it's much easier to consider ourselves subject to Him than to our all-too-human spouses.

Some women practice outward compliance with inward rebellion. God is not impressed. Be aware, too, that sometimes "submission" becomes a convenient dumping ground for resentment that actually proceeds from other causes. Take a keen look inside yourself and identify the sore spot(s). Are you angry? At whom? Perhaps you're even vexed with God, with the position He's given you. Talking it over with your husband, a trusted friend, or your pastor can help you sort things out. Often just discovering the root cause, naming it, and deciding to let it go will dissipate the rage.

Most important of all, if you're feeling resistant and resentful, confess your feelings to God in prayer. Be assured that God understands, because He knows that we're sinful human beings (Ps. 103:14). Ask Him to cleanse you and to fill you instead with His peace. Don't expect an instant change of heart;

this is usually a learning process that takes some time. As you continually surrender to the lordship of Jesus Christ in your life, you become increasingly willing to yield to Him.

It helps if we remember that it's *not* weakness when one yields by choice. Indeed, haven't you noticed that only insecure people feel it necessary to remind others of their power and authority? Only people with frail egos consider the one giving direction more important than the one taking it. True strength comes from within—from knowing who we are and whose we are—not from standing up for our own interests.

The Christian marriage always has been unique. As society becomes increasingly self-centered, the contrast is more clearly defined. For within this God-ordained relationship, there is no rank. Each spouse is to submit to the other out of reverence for Christ. That's the framework for all relationships among Christ's followers, but especially for that between husbands and wives.

> [Jesus said:] "My command is this: Love each other as I have loved you. Greater love has no one than this, that he lay down his life for his friends." (John 15:12–13)

Jesus loved us not for what He could get but just because He loved us. As marriage partners, each of us lays down our life in serving the other—though sometimes one or the other may *seem* to be giving more. Each ministers to the other—not by law but by love.

"I've been chided for giving in too easily and moving when my husband has a job change," says Hazel. "True, those frequent moves limit me, even though I'm good at what I do. Such comments always give me pause . . . and set me right back to my personal priorities. I have a wonderful relationship with my husband—and isn't that what everyone is looking for? So if I lose some of my 'rights' by putting him first—and thereby keeping our relationship strong—who's suffering?

"Marriage can never be 50-50," she continues. "If you accept the husband's role as head of the household as a 'given,' then the wife's career falls automatically into a secondary slot.

We've seen several 50-50 marriages fall apart, simply because the couples were preoccupied with who-ought-to-do-what. If you really love someone, who keeps track?"

Love Thy Neighbor

Christ gave us two principles to live by, saying that all of the Ten Commandments are fulfilled in these two:

> "Love the Lord your God with all your heart and with all your soul and with all your mind." This is the first and greatest commandment. And the second is like it: "Love your neighbor as yourself." (Matthew 22:37–38)

Who could be a closer neighbor than our husbands, with whom we share a life? In that life together, husband and wife are in union, yet individual. Separate, yet equal. Indeed, for those who believe that God placed women in an inferior position, it's worth noting that in Genesis 2:18, the Lord God said,

> It is not good for the man to be alone. I will make a helper suitable for him.

The Hebrew root word for helper means to surround; to protect or aid; to help or succor. It has the same root as that describing God Himself in Psalm 46:1:

> God is our refuge and strength, an ever-present help in trouble.

Picture a relationship of two partners who support each other as friend and ally. Picture two people who know absolutely that each can count on the other, no matter what. Male and female—husband and wife—are two parts of the same whole, alike yet different.

So again it comes down to a decision. Each of us needs to ask ourselves: Whose standards will I adopt? Will I accept God's instruction? Grudgingly or gladly? How do I elect to live my life?

> But we are meant to speak the truth in love, and to grow up in every way into Christ, the head. For it is from the head

that the whole body, as a harmonious structure knit together by the joints with which it is provided, grows by the proper functioning of individual parts, and so builds itself up in love. (Eph. 4:15–16 Phillips)

That description of the unity of believers applies to husbands and wives particularly. After all, don't we "individual parts" want a "harmonious structure"? Christ's love lights the way:

Be imitators of God, therefore, as dearly loved children and live a life of love, just as Christ loved us and gave himself up for us as a fragrant offering and sacrifice to God. . . . For you were once darkness, but now you are light in the Lord. Live as children of light (for the fruit of the light consists in all goodness, righteousness and truth) and find out what pleases the Lord. (Eph. 5:1–2, 8–10)

Yet living and loving as His people is a formidable task. Sometimes—often!—it goes against our natural inclination. But the Savior does more than issue edicts. He who created us and knows us best also empowers us by His Holy Spirit.

May the Lord make your love increase and overflow for each other. (1 Thess. 3:12)

So even though we don't understand God's reasoning, we can abandon the struggle and rebellion—and relax. We can rest calmly in the sure knowledge that our Creator does all things well.

We are free to rely on Him, to help and support each other, to love, to enjoy each other, to serve each other—to grow together in our marriage relationship. The place of submission, rightly understood, is meant to be a place of deep, lasting fulfillment and gladness—the place of wholeness.

The best advice I can give to unmarried girls is to marry someone you don't mind adjusting to. God tailors the wife to fit the husband, not the husband to fit the wife. (Ruth Bell Graham)

4
Living with Your Husband

Marriage resembles a pair of shears, so joined that they cannot be separated; often moving in opposite directions, yet always punishing anyone who comes between them.
      —Sydney Smith

When I consider our marriage in comparison to that of our parents, I rejoice that we communicate so much better. Maybe that's because we don't have areas marked 'his' or 'hers.' For us, it's been 'Good-bye, little woman; hello, partner!' And we like it that way!
      —Husband

Ten years ago I married a secretary. Now she's a district manager and I'm the boss's husband. I finally understand why corporate wives feel like nonpersons at company functions.
      —Husband

He's proud of me, not intimidated. But I'm careful not to rub in the fact that I earn more.
      —Wife

After years of hard work, I can finally work shorter days and take long weekends. Time off—what Gayle always

nagged about. Now she's pouring herself into her career, bucking for a promotion. So I have all this free time for myself, I guess.
    —Husband

Today's husband may occasionally wish he had a traditional wife leaning on his arm. Most recognize, however, a clear gain in having a wife who's a fellow wage earner.

"I look at it this way," says Mike. "Maureen carries part of what would otherwise be all my responsibility. The leaky roof, a new transmission for the van, orthodontia for Nathanael—they'd all land in my lap. So I feel less burdened than some guys I know. If I were injured or laid off, we'd still have one paycheck. And I've finally gotten it through my thick skull that I don't have to have all the answers, that I can admit to Maureen when I'm scared. That's a relief!"

The two-paycheck couple often shares a true sense of partnership in all areas of life. That includes parenting their children. For instance, today's typical father likely spends more time with his children than did his own father.

"I'm a lot closer to my kids than my dad was to us," Mike continues. "I coached Maureen at their birth and held them right away. I changed their diapers and gave them baths. They're in school now, but I help them with homework. We play ball, go camping . . . And I love it. I think Shannon and Nathanael are the neatest two little people in the world!"

Exhausting though it is, the two-career life-style provides its own unique rewards. Women often think that they work only for the paycheck, but there are less obvious payoffs.

"I feel good about me," says Maureen, age 34. "I like pulling my own weight. And every day—want to or not!—I'm forced to stretch. If I were still at home I'd probably still be majoring in TV. Have to take care of myself, too; the woods are full of sharp, attractive gals, many of them younger.

"These days I love coming back to this house at the end of the day. But I used to mentally redecorate this place every time

I bought a new magazine. I was never satisfied!" Maureen says, smiling. "Now I haven't time to sweat the small stuff.

"Guess that applies to the kids, too," says Maureen. "Our time together is limited and I don't want to mess it up. So I save the hassles for honest-to-goodness wrong behavior, rather than losing my cool when someone spills a glass of milk or comes in with muddy shoes. And I think our children are actually better off. They *know* their father. There's nothing I do for them that he couldn't—or doesn't. That's a plus for all of us."

But there are trade-offs, too. Leisure becomes mostly a wistful memory. Of necessity, whichever wheel squeaks most loudly gets attended to. So long walks, lazy afternoons, lingering conversations in front of a toasty fire remain, for the most part, among the missing. All the week's allotment of 168 hours is spoken for, well in advance. And because of the pace at which they live, marriage partners exhaust their energy—emotional and physical—taking care of the "musts." So their marriage relationship gets the bits and pieces, the scraps.

Yet why should that surprise anyone? Think about it. Every human being has a limited amount of physical endurance, mental concentration, and emotional strength. Both spouses work long days at occupations that demand their best efforts. Their performance is closely monitored. So they may come home wanting nothing more than to be left alone, to lick their wounds after the day's battle. They simply cannot handle one more demand. It's an understandable reaction to stress, which has been called our time's universal disease.

Find Your Own Way to Cope

A lot depends on individual chemistry. For some working couples, especially those in high-pressure jobs, weekday evenings are a wipeout. "We just crash," says Holly. "We unplug the phone, eat something quick in front of the TV, and often don't even talk—don't write letters, don't call our families or friends. All day we talk on the phone; at night we want peace and quiet!"

That's not necessarily an unhealthy attitude. People who give their all during the workday need to wind down and replenish their energy for tomorrow's repeat performance. They may consider weekends their opportunity for togetherness. Perhaps this describes your marriage. If both of you are content with your arrangement, there's no problem. If one of you objects, however, you need to negotiate a balance both can live with.

If your relationship seems colored dull gray, consider that a symptom, not the disease. Look deeper. For example, if a husband or wife always pleads exhaustion when the partner wants to make love, fatigue isn't the only problem.

The success of marriage lies in creating a real bond of emotional closeness. Where that exists, partners freely bestow ego strokes, for each is secure. Their mutual trust frees them to discuss potential difficulties unafraid. Because they accept each other unreservedly, their communication is uninhibited. The two are partners in every sense of the word. In such an atmosphere, problems shrink to manageable proportions.

Some would say that description sounds suspiciously like pie in the sky. But have you read 1 Cor. 13 lately? Of course, no one achieves perfection in marriage. Yet countless couples do establish and enjoy enduring, satisfying marriage relationships. The secret lies in remembering that the husband and wife are two-thirds of a trio. The third member is God, who laid down the pattern for Christian marriage. *He* is the foundation for our home and the source of love. And He lives within us, gently guiding, molding, and (best of all) empowering us.

Know Where You're Going

Are you moving toward a goal? Or are you just moving?

Whether you've thought about it or not, as an individual and as a couple, you're on your way to somewhere. Will the course you're on take you where you want to go? If not, how do you get from here to there?

A lot of us hate plans. We cling to an illusion of ourselves as romantic, spontaneous creatures of impulse. Planning sounds so dull! Yet unscheduled time tends to dribble away when we're not looking. Or as one poster says, "Life is what happens to you while you're making other plans."

So it's important that both of you understand yourselves—and each other. Only then can your objectives be meaningful. That discovery can't be completed in an afternoon. But God's Holy Spirit can help you to peel off the masks and see within—if you ask. Barriers put aside, true communication begins.

At least every couple of months, reserve a chunk of time to rethink your progress and aims. Don't assume that you know where your partner is today just because you knew last month. Without mutual planning and regular evaluation, you're almost guaranteed to end up where a lot of couples find themselves: out of sync. That's a prime source of conflict in marriage.

"Why does Chuck always make extra demands at the exact moment I'm most overloaded in my job?" moans Celia. "I knock myself out to get established in this position—which has a terrific future, by the way. You'd think he'd understand. But no; he expects me to be able to take vacation days or quit early, just because *he* has some slack in *his* schedule!"

"Plan your work and work your plan," say the experts. "Then you can accomplish all your major goals." Well, sort of. You and your husband may carefully plot your workdays and weeks. Yet you're inevitably pulled in separate directions. One will have an opportunity for time off or for a business trip, while the other frantically works overtime to meet a deadline. One will be experiencing pain and yearning for extra evidences of love, while the other, absorbed in a project, remains oblivious.

Low-level internal conflict is a given. Each of you struggles to participate fully in your relationship as well as to succeed on the job. Often, because of time pressure and unrealistic expectations, you wind up feeling that your performance in both arenas is inadequate.

Be Forewarned: Transition Escalates Stress

When one partner in the two-career marriage changes careers or employers, both spouses face adjustment and added strain for awhile. A partner coping with new job responsibilities, pushing to prove capability at work, "lets off steam" at home. The spouse experiencing shaky job security or in the midst of unemployment desperately needs extra tenderness and support. Yet all the while that person exudes bad temper or withdraws or sinks into depression, none of which is endearing. Wise marriage partners strive to maintain their own emotional equilibrium, so they have something left to give to their hurting mate. In a nutshell: Try to avoid both of you being in transition at the same time.

Another source of conflict is that husbands and wives come into marriage with two separate sets of preconceptions. Their attitudes—and their expectations—will likely change over the years.

A frequent out-of-sync situation arises when the children leave home. The empty-nest couple often wants different things from life. The husband, who earlier endured endless overtime work, night classes and perhaps frequent transfers, may finally have come within sight of his lifelong goal—and he likes the view. At last, he reasons, he can relax the pace; now the couple can travel and enjoy life.

His wife, on the other hand, senses a lack of purpose with her children launched and embarks on a new course. Anxious to prove herself, she eagerly puts in extra hours and brings work home. After all, she can devote single-minded energy to her job now and hasn't got forever. She finds the pursuit exhilarating. Her husband remains unimpressed.

"Roger doesn't take my job seriously," complains Ellen. "He views my job as a nice little hobby, but with pay. He's always saying, 'Well, you don't *have* to work, you know.' But I don't intend to give up my job. My family has always appreciated me for what I do for them. But at work I'm just Ellen, and they value my contribution—period. My work means as much to me as Roger's does to him. Why can't he see that?

"I know he wants to travel now; isn't that ironic? He never had time for vacations when our boys were growing up. We took a week off a few times, but he fidgeted the whole time. I don't want to go away together on long trips. I don't even know what Roger and I would talk about . . . "

Roger has an opinion, too. "Ellen always knew what we were working for. Now we've arrived, and I can ease off. But where is she? Off in some nickel-and-dime job! I married a woman who would always be there. I come home tired at night, expecting a good dinner and some companionship. Instead I sit at the kitchen counter and eat a TV dinner or a carry-out pizza because she's pooped. I'm as good a sport as the next person, and I can live with fast food once in awhile . . . but I didn't knock myself out all those years for this. And I don't intend to start cooking and cleaning at this stage of my life, either!"

Both have some validity in their points-of-view, but they need to develop empathy. Then Ellen would understand that when Roger reminds her that she needn't work, he may be reassuring himself that he's still capable of being the bread-winner. He may feel threatened because her new confidence has led him to wonder whether one day she'll decide that he's surplus baggage. These may be the thoughts that wake him in the middle of the night with a churning stomach and a dry throat.

On the other hand, Roger may have the traditional roles so ingrained as the "right" way to live that any change would make him feel that he (or Ellen) are somehow sinning.

Telling Roger he's "just being stubborn" won't help. Ellen needs to communicate her search for fresh meaning in her own life. Once he realizes that she's out to prove to herself (and everyone else) that she's not "over the hill," his turmoil will probably lessen, freeing him to be more supportive.

Change in One Means Change in Both

In marriage, when one partner changes, the other must accommodate, whether by choice or not. Loving negotiation is required. Each of us resists change, yet situations that demand it keep coming up—all through life. Unless we manage to reevaluate and adjust, a rift may develop.

For example, one partner shifts hours or employment, so the other must adapt. Sometimes the factors are more subtle. Consider the marriage partner who takes night classes for a degree, becoming well versed and conversational on a topic that is little known to the other. When either partner feels like a "have" or a "have-not," the relationship shifts slightly.

Even a salary raise calls for adjustment. Suppose the mate with the higher paycheck dreams of fulfilling an expanded "want list," while the other insists that the added income be put away for the future. Or one partner may judge that the wage hike signals a move to a more expensive neighborhood, while the other wants to stay where they are.

Upwardly mobile executive couples, too, sometimes find promotions and salary raises a mixed blessing. "I'm sincerely glad that Mel's doing what he wants to do," says Greta, thoughtfully. "He's living out his dream. Terrific! Unfortunately, when he became the boss, *I* became the boss' wife. And frankly, I never fancied that role. Now I'm expected to be an instant superhostess and a sparkling conversationalist who remembers to 'mingle.' I have an image to live up to that I never aspired to!"

If Greta works through her resentment and concentrates on the positive aspects of her life, the two will likely grow closer. Outward acceptance with inner rebellion, however, guarantees an eventual explosion.

Beware Feeling "Stuck"

*P*erhaps the wife is working only because her husband's pay won't cover the bills. Low salary, unemployment, and/or an oppressive load of debt are common reasons. That's usually a struggle—for both.

"Sure, I know we're lucky that Darla could find a job," says Jeff. "My factory—the only one in town—closed down and left hundreds out of work. But that don't make it any easier! My dad brought me up to think that a real man takes care of his own family and don't lean on nobody for help. So what does that make me? Had no choice . . . my unemployment was running out, and the kids needed new clothes for school. When I see how tired Darla looks when she gets home from that all-night greasy spoon, I feel like a real loser. She shouldn't have to be on her feet all night!"

Many husbands share Jeff's feelings, no matter what led their wives to enter the labor force. Those in mid-life, especially, are likely to hold the traditional view: A Real Man is responsible for his family's basic needs. If the Little Woman wants a Little Job for "pocket money" or new furniture or to upgrade family vacations, he can accept that. But when his wife *must* work—to buy milk and eggs and school shoes—it shouts to all the world (he thinks) that he's inadequate in his primary role. Somewhere deep inside a persistent voice nags, "If you were a Real Man . . . ."

Childhood Memories Color the Present

Most of us consider ourselves more enlightened than previous generations. We've done enough reading and absorbed enough pop psychology to help us understand better what makes people tick. Yes, we agree, males and females aren't so different, after all. Roles needn't be so rigidly defined. We are, after all, thinking people!

Popular theory has it that times have changed and what women anticipate in marriage differs markedly from past generations. For both sexes, however, perceptions often are altered only on an intellectual level. The tune that plays in our subconscious has different lyrics. For example, the strongest influence—even when we didn't like it—is the role modeling of our own parents. Other significant people in our lives, books, and movies color our thinking, too. Consider the hours spent watching generous doses of TV sitcoms filmed in the 1950s. (How many reruns of "I Love Lucy," "Leave It to Beaver," etc., did you watch?) All those influences have fed our innermost image of how we "should" feel and function.

When our present actions contradict that old inner script, we have the sense that something's not quite right. So we grapple with a mélange of disquieting emotions. Satisfaction proves elusive. Even when a wife works by choice, her husband may feel diminished somehow.

The boy who grew up with an old-school father still retains that image. So if his wife is fully able to arrange for her own financial needs, if she leaves the house and operates superbly within a milieu unknown to him, he may feel that she is rejecting his contribution—or even that he, himself, is rejected.

A similar inner dictum plagues the wife who unconsciously models after her mother, who believed that a woman's highest calling was in her home. Even a thriving career fails to snuff out those bothersome doubts: "Am I all I should be as a wife? Are my children suffering?"

Understanding Those Childhood Scripts

Childhood messages intrude on today. Their effects often engender attitudes and behavior we find baffling. When we identify the forces that molded our husbands—and ourselves—the mysteries often vanish.

Begin by probing within yourself so you can recognize the basis for your own mind-set. Then pool your insights with those of your husband. Set aside your preconceptions and look at the world through your partner's eyes as well as your own. Here are some thought-starters:

● What picture of marriage did I get during my growing-up years?

● Does that help me understand myself and my partner better?

● Does that childhood perception fit my (our) present intent?

● What's my (our) current goal for our marriage?

● What kind of relationship do I (we) want to have?

● Does our life-style reflect our professed desires?

● Does our relationship exemplify our values and our Christian principles?

● Do I (we) need to make changes? If so, what are they?

Remember that the object of this laborious, perhaps painful procedure is *not* to remold either of you to fit the other's specifications. Rather, it's that each may gain self-awareness plus empathy for the other.

"The Warren I've known has always been a successful executive," says Judy. "He never wanted to talk about his childhood, so I dropped it. Lots of things I didn't understand—like why he's so tight with a dollar when he makes an excellent salary—and so do I. I used to rail at him, 'What are we working for, anyway? Why can't we just enjoy our money? Why can't we travel? Build a new house?' It was an endless dispute and we never resolved anything.

"Then we went to a marriage enrichment weekend and the walls came down. For the first time Warren let me see the pain of his childhood. How they'd lived in a rat-infested tenement. How they sometimes had oatmeal three times a day—and maybe not even that. He wept, and so did I. At last I understood what drives my husband—his fear and his need . . . so I can just let him be. At least we can talk about it now. We're working it through together."

To identify and understand each other's motives doesn't mean that either must remodel your own judgment to fit. In fact, the richness of the two of you together may be traceable to your basic dissimilarities of personality. Together you have a broader perspective—more facets to your coupleness—than if you were mirror images to each other. As you jostle each other with your differing outlooks, you round off each other's sharp edges. Think of rocks in a rock polisher. You shape and smooth each other into something far more beautiful, with much more depth, than you could have become on your own.

Higher Income Leads to Higher Outgo

If you're a typical dual-career couple, you almost certainly have more disposable income than if only one spouse worked. Probably you both relish the attendant extras (which somewhere along the line became necessities). So as the family standard of living inevitably rises, it becomes incontrovertible that one salary couldn't possibly maintain your accustomed way of life. What once may have been an option now becomes a permanent mandate. The truth is, you may be able to live on one paycheck, but the cutback would hurt. That's a simple fact.

You and I may protest that we'd actually love to quit and stay home, but we simply can't. So perhaps it bears reminding: all of life is a series of choices. If we're honest, we'll admit that we enjoy shopping in the "Better Dresses Department" instead of in the "Budget Shop." And don't we all prefer dining out to peanut butter and jelly sandwiches?

One thing leads to another—and we overextend ourselves. That may mean taking on extra responsibilities for extra pay—or for a more rapid career rise. It may mean that we mute troublesome misgivings about our children.

Let's get it straight: Being employed is not inherently negative. Appreciating nice things and having wider options in our lives isn't sinful. But each of us must grasp that our choices—whatever they are—have a lasting effect. Like chickens, they come home to roost. Today's decision leads to tomorrow's situation, and that process shapes our lives. So it's wise to take our eyes off today and ask ourselves, "What wheels will this particular action set in motion? Will I be pleased with the long-term results? When I look back from tomorrow's perspective, how might I view these alternatives?"

Think before you act—always. Weigh your alternatives by your long-term objectives. Be honest with yourself. Take responsibility for your life choices and your actions. If you find that you've become more acquisitive than you'd realized, confess it to the Lord and ask Him for an attitude adjustment.

I ## When He Insists That She Keep Working
n contrast to husbands who are threatened by working wives, there are also husbands who are angry when their wives do not work.

"When Maggie and I married, we had an understanding," fumes 28-year-old Brett. "We'd both work; we'd postpone having children until we had a nest egg saved. And even then she planned to take off just a month or so for maternity leave. She was crazy about her job! Vowed she'd come unglued if she had to stay home all the time.

"Everything went according to plan," Brett continues. "Two months ago she gave birth to Zachary, and we were on top of the world. But get this: She tells me she 'can't bear' to leave him and doesn't intend to go back to her job! I can't believe it— and I feel double-crossed. She knows we can't live the way we've been living on *my* salary. How am I supposed to pay the bills? How will we ever manage to buy a house? How could she do this? I feel as if I'm left holding the bag!"

"He wants me to leave our baby with a stranger! How could he ask me to do that?" asks Maggie.

Counselors report that they're beginning to see more and more young men who married, expecting that their wives would always be fellow breadwinners. These men feel betrayed—angry—if their wives, for whatever reason, quit working. They look at the inflationary climb in housing costs, and they feel overwhelmed if expected to provide for all the family needs. These men don't want an old-fashioned wife. They want a helpmate who helps meet the monthly bills.

"Oh, I went back to work," Maggie said months later, "because I *had* to. I couldn't stand forcing Brett to moonlight in a second job. But it's been rough.

"Believe me, I never expected to fall in love with motherhood. I can spend hours just watching Zach and feel total joy. But I did agree to help share the load, and I do like my job. It's just that when I'm at work I'm overwhelmed by loneliness. I want so badly to be home with my child!"

Couples like Brett and Maggie need to share their feelings and work toward resolution, perhaps with the help of a professional counselor.

G *Taking Turns Bringing Home the Bacon*

Giving each other a career break has become a growing movement. The wife, for instance, may do clerical work or wait tables so that her teacher-husband can open a landscaping service. Then, when that business is solvent, she'll quit her job and take a fling at being an artist. The husband may pay the bills so that his wife can get a beautician's license or advanced training. Once she's attracted a following, he may give himself a sabbatical and volunteer to help build a mission school. Some couples trade off regularly, enabling each to pursue further education or try out another job—or simply enjoy an extended break.

No matter how a pair structures the arrangement, the theme is, "Now it's your turn" (or "my turn"). The secret is that this gift must be given—and received—in the spirit of love.

Before resigning your job, however, examine your options thoroughly and resolve your questions/objections. Spell out exactly what each of you will do now—and when your positions are reversed. Decide on goals, immediate and long-range. Set a time limit, too. When you can count on a definite cutoff date, you're less likely to resent the sacrifice involved in being the sole wage earner.

When you're on the receiving end, tune up your sensitivity. Don't become so absorbed in your own interests that you take your partner for granted. Remember that your freedom to choose comes via the indulgence of your spouse, so be lavish with your love and support. Unsung heroes and heroines do exist, but they often get tired—and cranky.

Couples who've exchanged roles have a unique perspective. Both have been the sole support of the family and also the financially dependent mate. Conflicts will still arise from time to time, but greater empathy and understanding is almost guaranteed.

The system becomes somewhat more challenging, however, once your friends reach a more comfortable spot monetarily. When everyone you know eats mostly beans, too, and has bookcases made from packing boxes, who complains? But it can be unsettling when your peers are flying to Spain and buying expensive cars, while you still drive an ancient VW and feel lucky to afford a weekend camping trip.

Children alter the balance, too. When Junior needs antibiotics or new shoes, you can't postpone the expense. Trouble also looms when the receiving partner becomes so engrossed and exhilarated that the couple's relationship assumes a low priority.

"I didn't mind working extra hours and weekends," says Marcia. "After all, that was our agreement. But I hated the feeling that Kurt never even noticed. He lived on cloud nine, spending every minute in the lab. I might as well have been living at the YWCA. In all those months, Kurt never once said thank you. I didn't expect him to kiss my feet, but . . . . Anyhow, one day I said, 'This is it, Kurt. No more overtime. Good old Marcia has had it!'"

Even when both partners are willing and committed, re-evaluate regularly. People change, and so do their dreams and goals. Be sensitive to one another's feelings; ask outright, "How do you feel about this arrangement *right now?*"

F *Make Time Where There Is None*

or most working couples, there *is* no extra time. You must extract it from your killer schedule. Sometimes that's not as hard as you think, but it does require creative thinking. Don't miss readily available opportunities for togetherness—they're hidden right in front of your eyes.

• Set the alarm clock an hour earlier some mornings and share a leisurely cup of coffee. Read a few verses from Scripture and discuss how they apply to you and your life together. Pray about the day ahead. In the dawn's gentle light you may find it easier to share feelings. And sometimes you may want to wake early and not do much talking at all. Such early morning closeness will refresh you more than the sleep you miss.

• Couples who commute to work together often find that a built-in opportunity to keep current with each other. Again, it requires concentration and commitment, so most couples surrender their commuting time to surface small talk and listening to endless news reports.

• Are there household and outdoor tasks you could pay others to do? True, hired help doesn't come cheap, but subsidizing a teenager could pay big dividends. Provided you don't immediately fill the time with other tasks or commitments, you'll have less pressure and more time for the two of you.

● Some couples resolve the inevitable scarcity of time between them by going into business together. (Better know beforehand that you're able to work together and enjoy spending each day side by side.)

● Schedule occasional weekends away from home, too—sometimes as a surprise for your husband. In theory, of course, you should be able to achieve the same relaxed state of mind at home. In practice, however, one tends to look at the weeds that should be pulled or at the to-be-ironed accumulation. So a change of scene itself helps you to turn your attention to each other.

(*Note:* In case all this sounds too costly, either in effort or in cash, remember that it's always cheaper than the marriage counseling you may require later if you let your relationship deteriorate too far.)

Tuning In to Each Other's Worlds

Since you and your husband likely lead two separate lives during working hours, it's helpful to be familiar with the surroundings of each other's work. Try to meet some of the people with whom he spends his workdays—and vice versa. That makes for better comprehension when you discuss your jobs.

Sometimes you may wish you could restrict all "job talk" to the workplace, but it's almost impossible not to bring home your workaday concerns. After all, you spend one-third of your waking hours five days a week at your workplace. When you come home tense about a work situation, be honest. Tension communicates in one way or another. Both of you will be spared frustration by simply announcing, "I'm really uptight about my job today, and I need some time to unwind before I'll feel like talking." Otherwise you may "put on a happy face" and then explode over a trifle.

Give each other permission to "dump" the workday's accumulated load at the end of the day. It's not necessary for the other partner to comment or try to solve problems. Strive, instead, for active listening—that is, show by your responses that you hear. For instance, instead of responding "He probably didn't mean anything by that remark," say something like, "It sounds as if his remark really bothers you." Once you've both shared the experiences of the day (good as well as bad) and offered each other loving support, you can leave them behind and concentrate on your life together.

Watch *how* you "unload," however. A nightly gripe session, endlessly rehashing old complaints, simply etches the list more deeply into your consciousness. So as a general rule, be honest—but borrow from Pollyanna and look for the good. That old-fashioned practice can gradually lower your tension level. (And wouldn't that add a lot to the quality of life!)

Your Attitude Is Up to You

*E*ven if you're feeling overworked and undercherished at the moment, there are a couple of virtually foolproof ways to be satisfied. Here's the first: Lower your expectations. Avoid inflated dreams. Face your life as reality, for that's the bottom line. That's where you live.

Can you accept your husband as a unique individual? Accept him *as he is?* Can you accept yourself? Comparing yourself, your husband, or your marriage to others is like comparing grapes to grapefruit. Each person, each relationship, is one of a kind. Unconditional appreciation of what is can work wonders. And that attitude unquestionably removes strain.

That goes for the rest of our lives, too. Much of our continual hectic pace, for example, comes not from too little time but from constantly demanding more of ourselves than we can possibly do. So *we set ourselves up* to miss the mark. Frustration and stress inevitably follow.

The second key to contentment is related: Remember that your attitude always remains within your control. You and I *choose* how we'll respond in any situation. We *choose* how we'll view our lives.

Do you choose to feel irritated and angry—to dwell in a cage of frustration and self-pity? Or do you choose the freedom and release of saying yes to your husband and your life as is? Do you choose to keep your eyes on the muck and mire you may be slogging through or on the warm sunshine of God's never-failing love? Circumstances never have determined happiness—and never will.

(Be aware that loving hearts, sincere intent, and honest effort may not in the end resolve your differences in perspective. Issues that either one pronounces "petty" may continue to snarl your relationship. That's the time to abandon self-analysis and pride and to seek out professional counseling—while there is time, before hearts are locked and barred.)

People all over the country plunk down cash to be told the formula for a consistently positive attitude. Couples long for—and pay to discover—ways to ensure honest, open communication. The simple truth is that both are the outgrowth of choice, commitment, and continuing effort.

Love As Jesus Loves

Our call as Christians is to love and accept other people (especially our husbands) as they are. For isn't that exactly how God through Christ accepts us? Transformation is accomplished through the gentle, persistent tug of the Holy Spirit on a human being's heart and will. So although we may have a clear picture of what our husbands "should" be, our most effective tactic is to commit them to God and to remember that we, too, are flawed.

It's a matter of concentrating on what is rather than on what isn't—of walking life's pathway and seeing the stars in spite of a stone in your shoe. Whatever the deficiencies in your marriage (and in your husband), if he loves you and is dedicated to your life together, you already possess what countless women ache to have.

Marriage is to be the union of two people who cherish each other, warts and all. Be an affirmer in your marriage, and you'll be affirmed. Express your gratitude for what your husband is and does. After all, don't *you* like to be appreciated? And don't you respond in kind? (These principles apply to children, too.)

79

Again, the choice is yours—always yours alone. You can support your husband and build him up. Or you can cut his ego into tiny pieces and serve it to those hungry to finish the rest of him. Either way, you can accomplish most of the job with words.

Modern psychology espouses as a revolutionary discovery the power of words. But the writer of Proverbs revealed the same principle long ago:

> Reckless words pierce like a sword, but the tongue of the wise brings healing. (Prov. 12:18)

> Pleasant words are a honeycomb, sweet to the soul and healing to the bones. (Prov. 16:24)

Why not resolve that your words—from now on—will bless those around you? Take to heart the old explanation Luther gave to the Eighth Commandment: Put the best construction on everything.

You and your husband are God's gifts to each other. Give each other the freedom of no-conditions-attached acceptance. Then move on joyfully into the rest of your life together. For today is the stuff of tomorrow's memories.

The greatest happiness of life is the conviction that we are loved—loved for ourselves or rather, in spite of ourselves. (Victor Hugo)

By the grace given me I say to everyone of you: Do not think of yourself more highly than you ought, but rather think of yourself with sober judgment, in accordance with the measure of faith God has given you. (Rom. 12:3)

Love is not blind—it sees more, not less. But because it sees more, it is willing to see less. (Rabbi Julius Gordon)

Where there is no vision, the people perish. (Prov. 29:18 KJV)

In today already walks tomorrow. (Samuel Taylor Coleridge)

What a wonderful life I've had! I only wish I'd realized it sooner. (Colette)

5

Not Tonight, Dear—I Have a Headache

The quality and frequency of a couple's sexual relationship is not determined by the day's work.
      —Husband

Most of the men I know agree: Wives are often too tired at the end of a long workday to have any energy left over for sex. But on the other hand, they usually feel better about themselves . . . and that probably enhances their sexuality.
      —Husband

Our sex life suffers. . . . We're just too tired too often. Fatigue, pure and simple!
      —Husband

We kid ourselves that husbands and wives "turn on" and sex somehow "happens." Not true!
      —Wife

"Have you ever noticed that in the Gothic novels the hero and heroine are swept away on a wave of passion and have sex on a hillside, among the daisies?" asks Becky. "Matt and I can't even get together in our own bedroom! We're usually bushed by bedtime, so sometimes we steal away to our room while the kids are watching cartoons or something. Even then, I guarantee you that within minutes somebody will be pounding on the door and yelling for us to come quick. Maybe the dog has barfed on the carpet, or the toilet's overflowing, or somebody broke something. I tell you, it's a wonder we ever managed to conceive three kids!"

Dual-career couples face unique challenges to maintaining a nurturing sexual relationship. Fatigue, either low-grade or full-blown, is often a steady companion. Doing a day's work at home after a day's work on the job leaves little time—or energy—for anything but essentials. Sex may come to be an "extra"—recreation—to be worked in, if possible.

In earlier days, a wife was told she must "endure" sex with her husband and "bear it bravely, for it is woman's lot." That unfortunate mind-set has long since died. (Shall we all cheer?) Today's self-assured woman is freed from any perception that she must somehow justify being supported financially. She doesn't hesitate to announce, "I'm simply not in the mood," or "I'm too tired to even think about sex." She takes such autonomy as her inalienable right. "After all, we're not going anywhere. We'll both be here tomorrow night," the weary wife consoles her spouse as they sleepily kiss good-night and roll over. And time marches on.

A flourishing sexual relationship is possible. However, the couple achieves that happy state by nourishing it with TLC and time together. The latter, of course, is the stickler, for two-paycheck couples are universally short of that most precious commodity: time. Yet there are pluses to being a two-income couple. "Now that I'm working, I like myself better," says Ann. "I guess we don't have sex as often, but when we do it's because we're both in the mood. So as far as I'm concerned, quality makes up for quantity."

"I can't quibble with that reasoning," says Will. "Ann does put in long days at work—and so do I. But I can recover. When she's turned on, I rejuvenate in a hurry! Doesn't seem to work that way with Ann, though. When she's tired, I can't budge her. She's got a right to her feelings, of course . . . and she does pull her share of the weight in supporting this family. Our lovemaking is terrific—when we get together. But I sure would like to have sex more often than we do."

Many counselors maintain that this issue between two working partners may be less exhaustion and more another variation of who's-in-control. When either spouse "gives in," the other wields the power—becomes the sole determinator of when the couple will have sex. Obviously, that can only chip away at their union. Self-respect as well as mutual respect are vital factors comprising a healthy sexual relationship.

Relationship Builders

The sexual relationship is composed of many factors: desire, quality of communication, one's own image of oneself (not the same as self-confidence), time to concentrate on each other. All play an important role.

Frequency of sexual intercourse is only one facet of the physical interaction between husband and wife. Touching, kissing, and embracing all can (and should) occur in other contexts; they in themselves strengthen the couple's bond—and their sexual relationship, too. Rightly or wrongly, however, most people regard frequency of intercourse as the barometer of the husband and wife's total relationship. So how often a couple does—or doesn't—engage in sexual intercourse is hard to ignore.

Stop Passing Like Ships in the Night

When a husband and wife work conflicting hours, they face special problems. Their motivation may be to avoid leaving their children in day care, so she works the night shift and he the day shift (or vice versa). Such a couple may judge that the personal sacrifice is worth it—if the outcome is more secure children. Sometimes one partner works the night shift only because the pay is higher or because that is the only available job.

Whatever the reasoning, such a schedule complicates life (to put it mildly). Arranging time together requires creativity and determination, yet many couples manage it with flair.

"I work the swing shift, and Lil works graveyard," says Art. "So I get the kids up and have breakfast ready when Lil gets home. That's our family time, and we try to make it special. After the kids go off to school, Lil and I sit down with coffee and talk. Or we watch our favorite prime-time TV program, which we've taped the night before. Then she goes to bed . . . or *we* go to bed . . . and our sex life has never been better!"

Lesley gets off work and goes home to an empty house at 5 p.m., Monday through Friday. Mike works late afternoons and evenings making sales calls. "Since I'm bushed by the end of the day, I grab a snack and then go to bed and sleep for two or three hours," says Lesley. "When I get up, I handle any correspondence Mike left for me to do, maybe do some laundry or ironing, and check my clothes for the next day. When Mike comes home about 11, we have a quiet dinner. We talk about our days, maybe watch the late show or soak in the hot tub . . . or take lots of time making love. Next morning, I go to work and Mike sleeps in. Works out just great for us—otherwise, we'd only see each other on weekends."

So the message seems clear: If you and your husband are constantly passing each other on your way out of the house, don't try to operate as "normal" couples do. Instead, assess your schedules, think imaginatively, and *plan* your time together— even your lovemaking. For if you wait for the "right time," you may wait too long. Your sexual relationship may become a duty—a perfunctory ritual between two wearied spouses. When you leave your relationship to "take care of itself," you may be consigning it to terminal illness.

Give Yourselves Time for Emotion

As with all of life, a couple's sexual interaction is constantly changing. For example, as your children grow older, there's less and less time between your last child's bedtime and your own. So you always have an audience—one that grows more curious with each passing year. Many couples find that somewhat inhibiting. It's possible to reach a point where the prospect of lovemaking usually doesn't occur to either of you until you enter your own bedroom. Then sexual arousal and intercourse is expected to be accomplished speedily, so you can obtain your quota of sleep.

Yet human beings don't come equipped with a switch whereby one can flip on instant desire. Even though a husband and wife's lovemaking needn't be exotic or lengthy to renew closeness, it takes time to shift gears from the demands of the day to tenderness and total absorption in each other. Abrupt encounters, especially if customary, lack something. Physical release, yes. Nurturing to the relationship, not much.

So it bears mentioning again that the sexual relationship between a pair is part and parcel of their all-day, all-week total relationship. Remember how you communicated love and desire in the early days of your life together? It was as natural as breathing—a love pat in passing, a secret smile exchanged, a wink across a crowded room. Those now-so-easily-overlooked signals can still set the stage.

Tune Out the World

One or both partners may be dismayed to discover that over the years their sex drive has waned—or at least become easier to sublimate. In former eras, boredom and/or aging were blamed. Now it's recognized that a parched marital relationship and/or greater involvement with other pursuits are more likely culprits. For the sexual relationship is mental as well as physical and emotional.

"In the beginning it was just the two of us. We used to joke that we spent all our time in bed!" says Elise. "Now we both have so much on our minds that making love takes a back seat. Walt supervises a whole wing of the factory. That's with him *all* the time. And I worry about the kids. Will Elizabeth get over her cough, or does that 99° temperature mean that she's getting bronchitis again? Will Jay, our teenager son, make it home on icy roads without an accident? Does my sister's mastectomy mean that I'm at greater risk? All that stuff churns around in my brain . . . and sex just doesn't seem very important. I know that's not right . . . but that's the way we operate, I guess."

That's the way many husbands and wives "operate." Somehow spouses develop a "mañana" habit when it comes to nourishing their marriage relationship. "Tomorrow I'll find time for him (her). Tomorrow we'll do something together." But tomorrow never comes, and the two drift farther and farther apart. Two strangers in the same bed.

Elise and Walt decided to change. They outlawed discussing work, debating the budget, family problems, etc., except during the first two hours after work or during a prearranged time.

"Now we really try to shut that bedroom door and give each other our full attention," says Elise. "We realized, too, that we seldom thought about each other in a loving way anymore. It was always critical—like, 'Why do I always have to ask him to vacuum the carpeting?' and 'Why does she always forget to fill the car with gas?'

"So we agreed to try to 'think sexy' more often—to be more playful. Took us awhile before we got in the groove again. But now we look back and can see how we've changed. And what a difference in our love life!"

Tip to Success

If Elise and Walt remind you of your own marriage, your first priority is not to find a way to have sex more often. Rather, concentrate on nurturing your relationship as a whole and many problems will cure themselves. Begin by regularly planning frequent time alone with each other. Time to reestablish communication, to discuss together your priorities and goals as a couple. Time to relax!

When you're feeling warm and close, talk over any disparity in your individual desires and needs for sexual intercourse. Be aware that what seems a faltering sex life may simply reflect prolonged neglect of your total relationship. In that case, infrequency and lack of interest are warning signs.

However, it's possible—but relatively rare—that one of you may have a consistently low level of sexual desire that has nothing to do with the quality of your marriage relationship. If so, you both need to know that, face it, and then decide how to deal with the imbalance. That may include consulting a physician. Certain medical problems and/or some prescription drugs (some blood pressure medications, for example) can lessen the sex drive in both female and male, as well as cause male impotence. Although not necessarily common, if these side effects occur often enough, they warrant a checkup. Usually a change in medication is all that's required.

What's the Norm?

There is no "acceptable" standard for frequency of sexual intercourse between a married couple—at any stage of life. That's a joint decision, to be reached by each couple individually. If both of you consider your relationship mutually enriching and satisfying in other areas, and if you're both contented with your sexual relationship, you have no problem. It's only when one or both of you is troubled and/or unsatisfied that there's cause for concern.

(Should that be your situation, be aware that professional counseling can usually enable a couple to overcome their difficulty, often rather quickly. But *do not* pick a counselor from a classified ad! Get a referral from your pastor or your family doctor. And don't be embarrassed; *be proud* that you care enough to work together on your marriage.)

After a full day's work that required the best you had to give in energy, involvement, and intelligence, most people want to rest and recoup for the day ahead. At least that's the excuse we offer for frittering away evening after evening, watching whatever is playing on television. Let that be your regular diet of couple interaction, however, and your marriage relationship will sooner or later suffer from malnutrition.

The Pause That Refreshes

The typically frenzied timetable of the working couple allows little disposable time. Yet if you yearn for your sexual relationship to be a vital part of your life, you need to be alone together frequently—and uninterruptedly. That's a gift you (and only you) can give to each other.

You may complain that you're both so tightly scheduled that you can never do anything on the spur of the moment anymore. And that's probably true. Rather than bemoan the loss of spontaneity, why not replace it with something more reliable? Guarantee yourselves time to talk, long walks, visits with friends, even lovemaking.

"The marriage counselor said we need to schedule regular dates," says Sandy. "Ever hear of anything so silly or unromantic? I don't want Joe writing me in his calendar as if I were his Thursday appointment! I want us both to be in the mood when we go out, or we won't have any fun!"

You prefer to be swept away on a wave of passion? Well, good luck! Think it over. What merits space on your own appointment schedule? Isn't it the meetings and people you consider too important to trust to memory? For most busy people, what *counts* is listed on their appointment calendars and their To Do lists.

When you have an I-can-bank-on-it date, you can stand the sustained hectic pace of daily life. Other demands may seem more urgent, but in truth, nothing ranks higher than strengthening your marriage relationship. Let your commitment to couple time be so firm that you almost never allow anything or anyone to lead you to alter your plans.

Unhurried opportunity to focus on each other becomes the warm sun that brings forth tender green shoots of new growth in your sense of being truly one. Clearly, that requires more than a 15-minute coffee break.

So be creative as you plan how to nourish your oneness. Mull it over. Figure out ways to juggle your responsibilities. And don't leave it to chance! Slate a weekly date. Breakfast alone at a fast-food place or a brown-bag lunch in the park (with time to talk) can be as reviving as dinner at an expensive restaurant. Schedule a 24-hour getaway at a nearby motel and "kidnap" your husband after work. Trade off baby-sitting with another couple, either for an evening or a weekend. Go camping together; it's cheap, and a night out under the stars can put the light back in your eyes. Declare one or more evenings "early-to-bed night." Explain to your offspring that Mom and Dad need some time to themselves. (If you wisely begin this practice while your children are very young, they'll assume that all parents operate this way.)

Although getting away together can be pleasant, it's not essential. A change of mood is called for more than a change of scene. The goal is to reconnect, to focus on each other. This is your opportunity to glimpse inside your husband—and perhaps yourself, as well.

When your "interlude" arrives, adopt a leisurely approach. If at home, unplug your telephone or turn on your answering machine so you won't be interrupted. Agree to forego any judgment/criticism of the other's remarks; you want to create a climate where each can share thoughts and feelings freely, without hurry, without fear of being put down. Keep in mind that this private pocket of time has been carved out of your hectic schedules so you can concentrate on *each other* and your life together. Introducing other topics leads sooner or later to just another discussion session. (And what's special about that?)

Beware also of scraping away at old wounds. You're there to build each other up. Turn your attention to your husband's good qualities instead, and you'll probably receive like affirmation in return.

Time and talk and touching can work wonders in reestablishing some of that intimacy of spirit that seemed natural earlier in your marriage. You needn't draw up an agenda for conversation or buy a book on "new techniques." You might encourage a relaxed mood by turning down the lights and burning a candle or two. Soft music is a nice touch; so is a pot of coffee or tea. And although easy conversation can be enriching, sometimes it's enough just to hold hands or to hold each other close without talking.

Whatever form it takes, such quiet communication, so often neglected in the rush of daily life, nourishes your relationship— and often fuels your desire for each other. This togetherness itself may be all that's required to restore your sexual relationship to what pleases you both. (It bears repeating that your sexual relationship may differ—in intensity or in frequency of intercourse—from that of other couples, either in real life or as depicted in the media. That's not at all important. But it is vital that your love life nourish each of you individually and both of you as a couple.)

"I know it's not logical," says Amy, "but when things are good between Cal and me, everything else is okay, too. Somehow lovemaking restores us—heals us. Problems and worries seem to melt away, and for a little while, all's right with our world. So if you ask me if our lovemaking is important, I'll say a definite yes! That's why I'll never understand how it can be so easy to put off."

A Sign of God's Goodness

The sexual relationship between husband and wife is God's ongoing gift (Gen. 2:24). That precious gift can't evoke its potential of joy and bonding, however, unless awarded its rightful place in the marriage and carefully nurtured. If you're honest, you'll likely admit that you manage to accomplish what you consider essential and/or worthwhile no matter how packed your hours and days. So perhaps the question to ask yourself is, In my priority ranking, what significance do *I place* on our sexual relationship?

If your answer reveals you've been shortchanging your wife-husband relationship, decide now—while there's time—to rearrange your scale of values. Don't think of it as a favor you're doing your husband but rather as a present to both of you. Like Amy and Cal—and countless married couples the world over— you'll probably discover that the quality of all your life improves when viewed through the rosy-colored lenses of a mutually satisfying sexual relationship. So whatever it takes to achieve that delightful state, it's decidedly worth the effort.

> I won't need your kind caresses
>   when the grass grows o'er my face;
> I won't crave your love or kisses
>   in my last low resting place.
> So, then, if you love me any,
>   if it's but a little bit,
> Let me know it now while living;
>   I can own and treasure it.
> —Author unknown

We escape from our teenagers for a half-hour or so every afternoon. After work, before dinner, we head for our bedroom with a pot of tea and share our day. That's our special, private time. And sometimes . . . well, it takes awhile longer. (Wife)

God has set the type of marriage everywhere throughout the creation. . . . Every creature seeks its perfection in another. . . . The very heavens and earth picture it to us. (Martin Luther)

For this reason a man will leave his father and mother and be united to his wife, and they will become one flesh. (Gen. 2:24)

6

Housework: Somebody Has to Do It!

My husband thinks he shares equally in the housework. But he's totally unaware of many of the things I do around here that are absolutely necessary to keep this place running!
       —Wife

Husbands and children must be trained in all areas of home maintenance. At our house we make up a schedule for everything and clearly define duties. Then we write outside help into the budget for what we as a family can't do. But to keep from going bonkers, you just give up and lower your standards.
       —Wife

Housework is still a burr under my saddle, even after many years. I love my job and some days I work very hard. But my husband and family somehow consider my work "Mom's recreation." So they feel no call to pitch in and give the Old Girl a hand. I could understand it if I spent my days out playing golf or shopping; then I'd expect to carry the housework burden alone.
       —Wife

In the modern marriage, the modern husband and the modern wife share all things equally—even housework. So goes the theory. Reality, however, may be quite different.

Both will agree that the concept is fair, but some estimates peg the percentage of men who actually help around the house at about 25 percent. Indeed, the word "help" angers many working wives. When both partners are employed, these women feel both should share in home responsibilities. Whatever a couple's particular division of duties, most women face several hours of housework/child care after they return home from a day on the job.

If working wives and their husbands had their druthers, they'd both welcome someone—someone else!—to run the house, take care of the laundry and cleaning, prepare the meals, send birthday cards, care for the children, etc. Unfortunately, not many couples can afford outside help.

"I am tired to the bone!" exclaims Paula. "Jim and I have talked it over again and again, but nothing ever changes. He seems to feel little responsibility for housework and taking care of our children. He promises to change—and I think he means it at the time. But the changes never last."

Counselors note that such continued conflict over splitting up the housework remains one of the most common trouble spots in the dual-paycheck marriage. Work agreements may not help much because each spouse interprets them differently. Unfortunately, there's no absolutely perfect method of resolution. Rather, each couple must hammer out their own arrangement—and be prepared for frequent renegotiation—until they've found what works best for them.

Applaud, Don't Attack!

Whe a couple begins to share chores, they need one cardinal rule: Each accepts the way in which the other does a job. Wives, for example, often convey the clear impression that their husbands can't do anything right.

Think about it. Roy volunteers for the weekly trek to the supermarket. When he proudly unloads three bags of groceries, Fran announces, "That's the wrong brand of detergent!—Oh dear, look at the brown edges on this lettuce; I'm afraid that won't keep too well.—Roy, this sausage has garlic in it and you know I can't eat garlic!—Didn't you read the labels? Oh well, never mind, you'll learn."

Roy does not, in fact, do much that meets Fran's standards. Predictably, before long he mutters to himself, "I can't please that woman no matter what I do! Might as well quit! Still, what's fair is fair; I ought to pitch in around here. Fran works a 40-hour week, too."

So what happens as a reaction in some men? A piece or two of china somehow gets broken or chipped whenever they clean up after dinner. They make a sandwich and forget to put the leftover roast back in the refrigerator. They wash a load of white clothes and don't notice the red washcloth.

Unresolved Emotions
Are Often the Root of Problems

The name of this game is Sabotage—and lots of couples play it. Yet most husbands do not *deliberately* set out to sabotage the job. When Roy becomes suddenly forgetful, he's honestly oblivious of any connection with unexpressed anger. In fact, if you suggested such a link, he'd be insulted. Unresolved feelings, however, have a way of oozing out around the edges of our self-control.

Take Bill, for example. His wife, Karen, launched a career after 16 years of marriage. She's exhilarated by her paycheck—tangible reward for her efforts. Her new life-style invigorates her, even though she's also stressed and short of time.

Her husband, on the other hand, is less enthusiastic. It irks Bill to discover no freshly ironed dress shirts in his closet, no milk in the refrigerator for his breakfast cereal. Small things, yes, but from his perspective, a glitch in their life together that wasn't there before. Accommodating two work schedules has complicated his life.

Bill is truly proud of Karen. He loves her—wants her to be happy. Yet it's understandale if he occasionally longs for a return to their former life-style when she was more available to care for his needs.

His reaction isn't uncommon. Unable (or unwilling) to express ambivalent feelings openly, such husbands may give double messages that prove "crazy-making" to their wives:

"Another promotion? Terrific! I know you love that job." (Later) "Honey, I'm out of clean underwear again! That's the third week in a row!"

"Sure, it's only fair that we share the chores. After all, you work all day, just like I do." (Later) "Aw, Honey, I forgot to mop the kitchen again, didn't I? Don't know how that keeps happening."

"No problem about you working Saturday. Guess that's the price I pay for having a successful wife. I get to spend all my days off rattling around alone. But don't you worry about me— I'll find something to do."

Women give double messages, too. They insist that the couple's home belongs to both equally, so both partners should share in its upkeep. Then, like Fran, they make it plain that *they* set the standards within those four walls. In child care, too, the wife usually considers herself the authority, yet all the while she may be chiding her husband to take a more active role in parenting their children.

When marriage partners engage in these games, they're saying that they expect to have their cake and eat it, too. Impossible!

All of us, males as well as females, are picking our way down unfamiliar paths. We're often a bit uneasy, uncertain, even frightened. Some husbands, because of their own inner insecurities, feel threatened. They may lash out at their wives, but in a civilized (read that "veiled") manner. An intelligent man, after all, intends to be adult and logical. He may be unable to acknowledge, even to himself, that he occasionally hankers for a "clinging vine." All he knows is that his life is vaguely frustrating. Whatever your particular orientation toward handling necessary housework, if either partner uses or manipulates the other, you'll slowly strangle your relationship.

It's important not to let resentments smolder. Draw them out and keep on talking, even when you feel it's unproductive. Christian couples will want to incorporate the Scriptural principles of consideration and loving service.

H *Before Resolution, Find Understanding*

ow to handle the conflict? Unfortunately, Roy and Fran chose a common method of dealing with their situation. At first, she more or less patiently reminds Roy of neglected tasks and suggests more efficient ways to do them. After a while, she stops asking and takes over herself. Roy is off the hook but feels guilty. Fran seethes and feels betrayed. Between them lies a frozen expanse. Their sexual relationship, too, suffers from frostbite. Until they confront their situation together and honestly share what they're feeling, their mutual Ice Age will drag on.

Marty was wise enough to spot that same interaction developing in her marriage. Searching her heart, she realized her own contribution through her condescending attitude. "It was hard, but I confessed that to Jerry. He said when I remind him what to do, he feels as if he's a little boy again, and I'm his mother scolding him. I could have cried. No wonder he bristled! I asked Jerry to forgive me for being so insensitive. And I vowed to let him do things his way from that moment on, no matter what. Right then and there, I made up my mind to concentrate on his love. There's so much good in Jerry—but I could have driven him away because all I thought about was what he isn't."

One of our most important basic human needs is to be loved and accepted—as we are. That's uncomplicated reality. We females, however, tend to overromanticize most of life. Despite our no-nonsense attitude in our careers, many of us still retain remnants of a script left over from earlier days. It depicts a Prince Charming type who sweeps away every problem and lives up to every expectation. Sure, we recognize that we married imperfect human beings like ourselves. Nevertheless, the "if onlys" may linger in the corners of our consciousness. "If only he shaped up and pulled his own weight around here—as a husband *should*—my life would be so much easier." "Every other working couple splits up the housework 50-50. What's the matter with *my* husband?" In trying to remodel Mr. Average into Mr. Perfect, some of us become more a prodding parent than a supportive spouse.

Of course, the issue of housework looms larger than it should, mostly because it's daily and it's unavoidable. As with sand in the shoe, irritation over who does what can easily cloud perspective and overshadow the satisfactions in other areas of our relationship. Recognizing that housework—and any conflict connected with getting the job done—won't go away, how can we whittle it down to manageable size?

Set Your Own Standards

As one place to start, reassess what's important to you—*now*. You may be trying to live up to the housekeeping style of your mother—or your own style from when you were at home full time. Most working couples eventually decide that if they're to preserve their sanity, something has to give. Often that means lowering their standards of home maintenance. Engrave on your consciousness the principal that *a messy house is not necessarily an unclean house*.

You're not Aunt Cora or the lady down the street who makes a career out of shining her copper and waxing her furniture. Nor need you fear a visit from the White Glove Tester. Resolve, therefore, to concentrate on the basics. Begin by evaluating the various aspects of your life together. Decide together what you consider necessities—and don't overlook the art of elimination. For example, does your kitchen floor really need wax, or do you wax it out of habit? Could green plants that need watering every few days be replaced by others that survive with infrequent watering—or even by good-looking silk foliage? As a gauge ask yourself, Is this worth my time and/or expense?

With your spouse, agree on mutual standards. If you're to have a life-style that feels comfortable and satisfying to you, what's indispensable? One couple, for instance, may consider gourmet-type cooking not only a requirement but shared fun besides. For another, fancy cooking ranks with other time-wasters. One pair will insist that neatness is fundamental to mental health. Another will say, "As long as we can walk through the place and see out the windows, we ignore it."

I *Be Creative as You Divide the Work*

*I*f you're feeling overwhelmed—and perhaps a mite sorry for yourself because you feel you carry the major load of at-home responsibilities—there is a better way. Why not apply the same principles in home management as on the job? At work you can't afford to spend time fixing blame, nor can you verbally attack co-workers, either openly or subtly. Supervisors are sensitive to attitudes and know the importance of good morale—and eventually dismiss an employee whose operating style is destructive.

At home, your marriage may endure, even if one or both partners indulge in self-pity and continually attack the other with sarcastic "humor." But you'll be living in a desert wasteland.

God, however, intends you to enjoy the luxuriant oasis of mutual cherishing. The key to resolving your differences is to remove emotion from your discussions and determine, instead, to simply define the problem and decide how to deal with it. As one nonconfrontational method, list the tasks you've agreed are necessary to maintain your home and provide nurturing care for your children. Then set a time value on each task. (You can either guesstimate from past experience or do an actual time log by monitoring and recording time required to carry out daily chores over the course of a week or two.)

Next (as you would at the office), calmly discuss which "department" (spouse) will assume responsibility and trainability of personnel (as in a business situation). Remember that this is not to be a rundown of deficiencies but a realistic appraisal of which marriage partner is best suited for particular tasks. Institute a trial period with reevaluation set for a specified date.

As you prepare your list, divide home responsibilities into categories: housekeeping, family needs, child care. Then detail specific duties in each section to get an accurate picture. "Family Needs," for instance, is an umbrella term. Break down those needs into components. Here's a sample list. Adapt it to your own situation, as desired.

HOUSEKEEPING	TIME VALUE (min., hrs.)
• Daily housework (dishes, beds, general tidying up)	_____
• Preparing meals and lunches	_____
• Planning menus and grocery shopping	_____
• Wardrobe care (laundry, ironing, mending)	_____
• Periodic heavier housework (vacuuming, floor scrubbing, bathrooms, etc.)	_____
• Yard upkeep	_____
• Home repairs and care	_____
• Other	_____

CHILD CARE	
• Get children up and dressed	_____
• Chauffeur children to/from school and other appointments/activities	_____
• Assist children with homework	_____
• Get children settled for bed	_____
• Attend children's activities at school and church	_____
• Volunteer in children's activities (Sunday school, parent-teacher organization, 4-H, Scouts, Little League, etc.)	_____
• Schedule doctor/dental appointments, lessons, haircuts	_____
• Shop for and/or make clothing	_____

- Child two years to preschool age: Time spent reading, playing, comforting, bathing, etc. _____
- Infant under age two: Time spent feeding, bathing, diapering, etc. _____
- Other _____

TIME AVAILABLE	WIFE	HUSBAND
1. Time spent each day/week at work and in community		
2. Time spent in personal grooming, exercise, sleeping, etc.		
3. Time committed to church, necessary activities, leisure activities		
4. Time set aside to be together as a couple		
5. TOTAL HOURS IN EACH WEEK	168	168
6. Total hours already scheduled (add lines 1–4 for wife and husband)		
7. Total number of hours left over (subtract line 6 totals from line 5)		
8. AVAILABLE TIME		

Obviously, timing and recording your activities will cost you time and effort—but it can yield big returns. The completed list becomes a nonaccusatory vehicle for understanding. By reading it and participating in its preparation, both you and your husband will become keenly aware of your daily and weekly chores as well as of time limitations. You won't need to campaign for sharing the housework. This list provides logical, unemotional proof of the need for job sharing.

One caution: do not wave your list under his nose, yelling, "See? I *told* you I was overworked, didn't I? Yet there you are, taking it easy, while I . . . " Let the list speak for itself. Almost certainly, your husband didn't comprehend the minutiae of daily life and the time required to keep your family enterprise operating smoothly. (In fact, those conclusions likely surprised you, too.) So be gentle with your husband, be patient. Don't look for an overnight turnaround, but don't write him off as hopeless either. Be positive and accepting. Expect him to react in a loving way.

You've planted the seeds. Now water them with love and a prayer that the two of you can work through your differences. Gradually you'll settle on a division of labor that's comfortable for you both.

Find Your Own Style

How you accomplish what needs to be done is up to you. Some couples make firm assignments of tasks. In other marriages, each does whatever seems most urgent; the partner bothered by the sticky kitchen floor mops it. Then there are those meticulous pairs who devise elaborate rating systems. They award the least points to those chores deemed easiest or most desirable. The grubbiest jobs (which neither wants to do) earn the most points.

Some husbands and wives prefer to tackle a couple of chores every evening so that weekends are free. Others can't bear to do extra housework on week-nights; they save the whole list for the weekend. Some couples set aside one or two "Killer Nights" each week to accomplish weekly chores, again leaving weekends almost free for leisure and/or family. Under that system, when a chore nags at you during the week, you can assure yourself, "I'll do it on Killer Night"—and mean it.

Could you hire someone—a teenager, for instance—to come in and do the laundry or clean? How about the cooking? When considering your options, don't overlook senior citizens. You might gain a wonderful, cookie-baking grandparent substitute. Or look into having a live-in college student. (By the way, if you have grade-schoolers who think themselves too grown-up for sitters, someone who comes in during late afternoon hours would provide a face-saving means of after-school supervision.)

One of the unexpected benefits of being a dual-career couple is a heightened appreciation of home. As Marnie expressed it, "When I was home all the time, I was a cleaning fool. Even the woodwork was so polished it shone. And I wanted a new house so badly I could hardly stand it. Now I come home from work bushed, looking for peace and quiet. This old place looks pretty good to me after all."

Always Another Meal to Fix

*A*s for cooking, most dual-career couples already cut corners wherever they can. Try making a list of your family's favorite meals—foods that are quick to prepare or that can be cooked in advance, frozen, and then reheated. Aim for two weeks or a month of dinner menus. Then rotate these meals, using the list as a guide for shopping. When you feel creative, try out new recipes and add to your master menu those that make a hit.

Consider drawing up a master shopping list based on menu ingredients and standard staples; make copies and use as a weekly checklist for future shopping trips. Tackle the supermarket once a month. Buy a month's supply of staples, canned goods, detergents, paper goods, and freezer foods. Then each week or so, a quick trip to pick up perishables will be all you'll need.

A Saturday cook-in, where you work together to prepare food for the freezer according to your master menus, will make your Monday-to-Friday food preparation more relaxed. Some cooks also blend their own mixes and measure and bag dry ingredients. Expect a busy day—but if everyone cooperates, it can also be fun.

If you've gathered by now that it takes a lot of work to get organized, you're absolutely correct. Getting set up will seem laborious, but fix your mind on the reward: less stressful after-work hours five days a week.

The Secret of Surviving

*I*n housework, as in all other areas of your life, you can keep things running more or less smoothly if you're clear on what's essential to you both and stick to those guidelines. Pressure remains an inevitable fact of life for the two-career couple. You can't annihilate the stress, but you can keep it manageable.

Remove some of the mental strain by avoiding comparisons with what another woman accomplishes. She may have more energy on her worst days than you do on your best. She may function superbly on five hours' sleep per night, while you can't think clearly on less than seven. Learn the art of concentrating on the possible. Then shut your eyes to everything else!

And remember—with love and determination even housework can become a duet instead of a duel.

It is not doing the thing we like to do, but liking to do the thing we have to do, that makes life blessed. (Johann Wolfgang von Goethe)

Love is not only something you feel. It's something you do. (David Wilkerson)

A dairymaid can milk cows to the glory of God. (Martin Luther)

7

Children: The Big Decision— If, When, and How Many?

When I started working here, I was 24, fresh out of college, and newly married. One of the older women took me aside and said, "Let me tell you something I learned the hard way. Go home and have your babies now. You'll lose a few years that way—true. And when you come back, you'll start at the bottom. But if you wait a few years to have a child, you'll have worked your way up the ladder, and you'll have too much to lose."

Well, I didn't listen, of course. I wasn't ready to have children at that point. But she was right. Now I'm head of the department. People respect me, and I love my job. I can't bear to give it up! Yet I'm 35. If we're ever to have children of our own, we have to get going. Time is running out.

—Wife

Once upon a time, "marriage" and "baby carriage" not only rhymed—they were part of a whole. Children were perceived to make a marriage complete; bearing children fulfilled women, matured men. Babies were the matter-of-course accompaniment to marriage, often arriving on their own timetable. Faced with an unscheduled pregnancy, the typical response was, "We'll cope somehow." After all, hadn't generation after generation done just that?

Adults now in their childbearing years can't imagine a world without reliable birth control, a society where the very term was spoken in hushed tones. Yet in those pre-Pill days there was little choice and almost no publicity—certainly no advertising in the popular media. Christian couples struggled to determine whether limiting family size was God-pleasing. Hadn't He admonished Adam and Eve to "be fruitful and multiply"?

So hardly anyone thought to question the wisdom of having children. In fact, when a couple hadn't produced a baby within two years, friends and relatives usually deduced that they must have had a problem. Infertility, though not labeled the sign of God's disfavor as in Old Testament times, was judged to leave a void in the marriage.

(So if you've been getting some flak from parents and grandparents about starting your own family, tuck the foregoing away in the back of your consciousness.)

Married couples today often view children as an option. Most parents settle for one or two offspring. Many factors— some neutral and some negative—enter in:

- Contraception is reliable and considered medically safe.

- Over 50 percent of the marriages in this country are now dual-career.

- Expanded employment opportunities for women and changing technology make it mandatory to keep knowledge and skills up to date. Time off for bringing up children may be viewed as a liability.

- More women postpone childbearing until after they've become established in their careers, when fertility may be lower.

● We live in an era of self-fulfillment. Bringing up children, by its very nature, impedes absorption with self.

Consider All the Factors

Whether or not to have children is a decision for the two would-be parents under the direction of God. Arriving at a consensus can be a lengthy process. Talk it through in depth. Weigh what's involved, evaluating the positives and negatives.

Although modern thinking casually tosses aside God's command in Gen. 1:28, which clearly denotes parenting, Christian couples need to confront it. Remembering that God desires only the best for His own (and has not rescinded that original admonition), you'll want to consider prayerfully several other Bible verses that pronounce children a blessing, the gift of God: Gen. 4:1; 33:5; Ruth 4:13; Ps. 113:9; 127:3–5; Prov. 17:6. Also, your children, raised as believers in Christ, will continue Christianity as the salt, the preservative, of the earth (Matt. 5:13). Society will benefit from your children.

Incidentally, the decision to have a child in no way resembles the decision to build a house. You can't draw up a blueprint of your "dream child." Each comes into the world an unknown quantity, carrying genes and chromosomes that tie back into previous generations. It's not at all uncommon for parents to note that a child walks like Grandpa, has a temper like Aunt Ruth, and red hair like Great-grandma. And whereas building a house may cause a few arguments but likely won't alter the marital relationship, parenthood probably will—for better or for worse.

As you weigh the pros against the cons, you'll want to examine a multitude of elements. The following list isn't meant to intimidate, only to stimulate your thinking:

● Above all, study Scripture to discern God's will as it applies to your marriage.

● Evaluate yourself and your spouse. One is probably more the care giver, the other the caretaker. How will you handle possible changes in the balance?

- Know who you are individually and as a couple and what you stand for. Have a clear sense of your values and rank them in importance.

- Be sure that the determining factor in making your decision is your own emotion, not the judgment of others. Be aware, too, that if siblings or friends become parents, old rivalries may rise up to becloud your thinking.

- Think through your own view of parenting. What's in it for you? (Sounds selfish, but the harsh truth is that most of us expect some payback for our actions. It's better to discern that honestly beforehand, confront it, and evaluate that emotion.)

- How do you assess your own parent potential? Be honest.

- Observe the parenting styles among your acquaintances. The healthiest relationships come when parents perceive their children as individuals, unique and precious in their own right.

- Children need love, acceptance, and cherishing most of all. Are you comfortable expressing love in words and actions?

- Even in the best of circumstances, parenthood equals sacrifice. Do you have a servant's heart? Can your relationship survive occasional periods of neglect?

- Be sure that what you want is a full-time child. Your need to nurture could perhaps be fulfilled by volunteering to work with other people's children.

- You could "borrow a baby" from a friend for a few days or a week and get a superficial picture of parenting. But remember that "trying on" a baby inevitably remains an artificial exercise.

Keep Expectations Realistic

*I*n theory, of course, a child should not change anything. In fact, however, a baby changes almost everything. In theory, the husband agrees to share child care equally. In fact, that cannot happen. The mother who breast-feeds her infant, for example, can't say, "I took the last feeding; now it's your turn." Even when the child is bottle-fed, many men envision "child care" as cuddling a quiet, smiling baby or jostling a laughing toddler up in the air. A colicky newborn who screams incessantly or a six-month-old with persistent diarrhea seldom matches a husband's rosy view of fatherhood (nor a woman's dream of motherhood, for that matter).

If you expect life to go on as before, and if you anticipate avoiding conflict about alterations in life-style and in your marriage relationship, you're setting yourselves up for a fall. Even the most dedicated, most loving parents occasionally chafe at the added demands that children bring. Just because you *choose* to have children doesn't annihilate such human emotions.

A child ushers in the end of freedom, in a sense. As a parent you can no longer do what you please, when you please. Another human being depends on you, one who may not survive if you're not attentive. You're responsible for your child first—and then yourself—because you're the adult in this relationship. That's a sobering thought for some, invigorating for others.

This is not an argument against having children, but a reminder to be realistic. The couple used to acting on impulse, eating out frequently, dressing in designer clothes, and vacationing in exotic climes faces many adjustments.

The Age Factor

*D*ual-career couples often delay having children for any of a number of reasons. Meanwhile, the biological time clock, as it has come to be called, is ticking. Childbearing becomes high risk at some point, in spite of medical advances. These days, though, there's less fear associated with giving birth after age 35.

Certainly age is a factor. Fertility may be lower than earlier as the woman moves closer to menopause. The mid-thirties couple who discovers a previously unrecognized fertility problem has less time to work it out. The risk of miscarriage is somewhat higher, as is the risk of birth defects, particularly Down's syndrome. In spite of those factors, many physicians regard the healthy female who receives good medical care before and during pregnancy as facing little more risk than a younger mother-to-be.

More and more women are giving birth to their first child in their mid-thirties and beyond, having devoted their earlier years to becoming established in their careers. Some researchers call it a national trend. There is, after all, what's been dubbed "baby hunger"—the inexplicable inner yearning to bear a child. That longing strikes the female president of the board just as keenly as the stenographer in the typing pool.

"I wouldn't have believed it if I'd read it in a woman's magazine," says Antoinette. "I mean, here I am, 37 years old, president of my own company. Charles and I are free to travel, to change plans on a whim, to come and go as we please. I've always relished living the good life. But lately something has come over me. I see babies everywhere! I find myself wandering through the infant departments in stores. I have this sensation that time is running out, and that if I miss having a baby, I'll have missed out on the most worthwhile experience in life.

"Isn't that ridiculous?" she continues. "I've pitied my sister, Ellen, who's tied down with three small children in the suburbs. I've even told her that she's wasting her life, that her brain will turn to oatmeal! And yet . . . now I look at those beautiful kids, and I envy her. Still, a child or two would turn our comfortable world upside down. I don't know if I'm ready to abandon our free-'n-easy life-style."

There is another clear advantage for the older couple, aside from job and probably financial security. They're more mature; they usually know themselves and believe in themselves. If they've been married awhile, they also understand each other better and trust their time-tested relationship, having resolved the standard early conflicts. That frees more emotional energy for bringing up children—and like all other parents, they'll need all they can muster up.

Don't Go Overboard

*B*e aware that couples who become parents later in life seem especially susceptible to one weak spot: They sometimes lose perspective. For example, the typically more affluent parents may spare no expense. Designer-label diaper covers and stretch sleepers become standard equipment. They seek to ensure that their offspring shall have "all the advantages."

But it goes beyond economics. Some older parents revolve their entire lives around their children. Outside relationships and interests are neglected. Baby occupies center stage. (This goes beyond the humor involved when parents want to show you their slides, their videotapes, etc., and have one anecdote after another.) Later, such youngsters will probably be enrolled in an extensive program of after-school lessons and sports training and, of course, "the best" summer camps. These parents try to live out their own childhood dreams through their offspring. Ignoring the child's personal likes and dislikes, they force-feed the activities they themselves yearned for as children. Some attack parenting with the same zeal and efficiency they apply on the job. Parenting becomes a project with goals and time limits.

Doting parents aren't automatically harmful. The main hazard is that their youngsters may grow up expecting that life will always provide just what they want. The child who seldom hears an enforced no will grow up socially/emotionally handicapped. Privileges and possessions never equal love to a child. Children derive their emotional security from the certain knowledge that they're loved unconditionally and can count on parents for stability and support—and clearly communicated limits.

Parenthood: The Sacrifices and Satisfactions

*I*n an earlier era, denying oneself for a worthy cause merited praise. Self-sacrifice strengthened character; that alone justified any inconvenience or hardship. Parents willingly set aside their own wants and needs to provide for their children. They were, after all, raising a family—and nothing had more lasting value.

Today, admonished on all sides to stand up for our personal rights, our society has adopted a narrower view. Many consider it stupid to talk of denying oneself—for just about any reason

110

(except, of course, to lose weight). Research has proven, we're assured, that our first priority (our duty!) is to grow as individuals—to give ourselves every opportunity. If we're not well rounded, if we don't balance our life with ample doses of leisure and learning, we'll never fulfill our potential—so we're told.

There is, of course, some truth in that point of view. Unfortunately, many people take it too far. In the interest of self-actualization, they've become self-centered or, to use an old-fashioned word, selfish.

Indeed, if we aim to reach the limits of our capacity, rearing children can lead us there. As mothers and fathers we're stretched to our limits and become more than we'd be if left to ourselves. Yesterday's slogan rings true today: Children bring out the best in their parents.

Forced to get outside our own egos—to sublimate our own desires and focus instead on an insistent youngster—we unavoidably learn to give. Required to cope with countless new crises, we develop creative thinking and resourcefulness. Pressed to perform, even when we'd rather not, day after month after year, we solidify into people of integrity and reliability. We're enlarged as persons.

In fact, many people report a shock of recognition when they become parents. "It's as if a host of unanswered questions suddenly became clear," said one woman. "I felt someone should have announced to me, 'Welcome to the human race.' "

Children Enlarge Understanding

Most of us recall our own parents solemnly pronouncing, "You'll understand someday, when you have children of your own." It seemed another of those handy, unfathomable riddles that parents tossed around. Yet as our own children grow over the years, we do indeed comprehend life more fully. We learn about ourselves, our attitudes, our strengths—qualities we weren't aware we possessed. Perhaps those attributes develop within us as a response. But one thing is sure. As parents, none of us remains the same person we would have been without children, whether those youngsters come to us by birth, by adoption, or by marriage. We become mature.

The apostle Paul often spoke about Christian maturity. Gal. 5:22–23 lists the evidences that demonstrate that Jesus Christ lives in us through the Holy Spirit: love, joy, peace, patience, kindness, goodness, faithfulness, gentleness, self-control. All are the outgrowth of being rooted and growing in Christ. Those same qualities mark the fully developed character—and the years of parenting provide countless occasions for on-the-job polishing of those qualities.

Paul also indicates, however, that we consciously choose our outlook and our response to life. The stable personality is as much an act of will as anything. Paul gives us a short course in human relations in Col. 3:12–16:

> Therefore, as God's chosen people, holy and dearly loved, clothe yourselves with compassion, kindness, humility, gentleness and patience. Bear with each other and forgive whatever grievances you may have against one another. Forgive as the Lord forgave you. And over all these virtues put on love, which binds them all together in perfect unity. Let the peace of Christ rule in your hearts . . . . Be thankful. Let the word of Christ dwell in you richly.

Notice the action verbs: *clothe yourselves, bear with, forgive, put on, let.* They all indicate an intentional act. Paul mentions no conditions we can use as excuses. The message is simple and straightforward: This is how God's people are to live, so do it!

Those verses could have been written just for parents, for they address traits needed every day. But with or without children, we want people to recognize by the way we interact with them that we're emotionally balanced. When we live as Paul suggests, we project that personality. It originates in our union with the Savior, and when we consciously commit to grow up in Christ (Eph. 4:14–16). Drawing on His strength, we can meet the daily challenges of parenting with confidence. What we give up will fade from awareness as we savor the satisfaction of watching our children—and ourselves—grow up.

Don't Pressure Your Partner

Some men and women make it very clear before marriage that they absolutely do not want children—ever. Hormones and rose-colored glasses dominate the scene, however, and the prospective partner may think, After we're married that attitude will change. I know it! You may be in such a marriage right now. Perhaps you realize now the enormity of what you promised, and you've begun to long for a child.

At some point your lobbying may finally win an unenthusiastic assent from your husband. But that will be no victory, for there's no true agreement. The appearance of an infant is unlikely to mystically elicit unlimited love and dissolve forever those walls of resistance.

"I was positive that Earl would melt when he held our baby in his arms, but I was wrong," says Joanna sadly. "Oh, he loves Jason, I know that. But this is *my* baby and *my* responsibility. If Jason has a fussy night, Earl says, 'This baby was your idea, remember? You vowed that if I agreed to this child, you'd see that I was never inconvenienced. And frankly, I think walking the floor at 3 a.m. is a definite inconvenience. Hope he settles down soon.' And then Earl rolls over—and something dies in me. He's right, though; I did promise exactly that.

"As much as I adore our son, our marriage relationship has gone downhill ever since he was born," Joanna continues. "Yet I wouldn't have missed little Jason for anything. So I don't know where we'll end up. I guess I manipulated Earl, and now he's manipulating me. Down deep I'm afraid that I've gained a son and may eventually lose my husband. That really tears me up, because I love them both."

Joanna ignored the unmistakable warning signs. You may face a similar situation. So do not proceed with plans to have a child:

• As an attempt to strengthen a faltering marriage. (You need a secure relationship *before* adding the stress of child-rearing.)

113

- If you have lingering reservations whether a child will jeopardize one or both partners' rise in a career—and aren't sure how you'll deal with that.

- If one of you is lukewarm or even neutral about parenthood but "willing to go along with it."

- If either or both of you have a problem yielding to the needs of another person.

- If you're capitulating to continued pressure/longing from your own parents or see a child as a means of proving yourself.

- If you're a person (couple) who insists that matters should be done your way, who must maintain a certain standard, who finds it hard to adjust to sudden changes.

If any of those descriptions fit you or your husband, it's crucial to work through these feelings *before* starting your family. Seek out professional help if necessary. Would-be parents need a well-grounded relationship beforehand to avoid future problems.

"But I Can't Be Pregnant!"

*L*ife, however, is seldom ideal. Even in this age of modern technology, no birth-control method is foolproof (except abstinence), so unplanned pregnancies still occur. Perhaps right now you're confronted with that circumstance. Perhaps anger—even panic—churns within you.

Rest in the certainty that God can melt away your resentment, your doubts, and your fears and fill you with peace. And He will. But something is required on your part, too. You need to go before Him, honestly confessing the emotions with which you struggle. You may be reluctant to admit them to another human being, but be assured that God spotted those feelings from the beginning. Why not speak them out and lay your turmoil at Christ's cross? Ask His Holy Spirit to give you a new heart (Ps. 51:10). God promises to forgive you at once, once and for all (1 John 1:7, 9). Nevertheless, your "heart transplant" will likely be a gradual process. Yet if your continual prayer is that God will change your attitude, you can depend on Him to do so.

For those having second thoughts about a pregnancy, some would consider abortion a simple, obvious solution. The topic isn't germane to this book and won't be discussed. Just for the record, Christians never consider abortion a desirable option. Ps. 139:13–14; Job 31:15; 33:4; and other Bible verses clearly illustrate the significance of the yet unborn.

If you're pregnant and it was unintended, ask the Lord's strengthening. Resolve to abandon the "what ifs" and trust God to meet your needs. Take the positive approach; *choose* to accept this child as a special gift from God. Parents who've shared this experience almost always relate that their "bonus baby" proved to be a unique blessing. Yours will, too. Be assured that our all-wise God still orders your steps; He already knows that tiny infant growing within you. Rest in that knowledge and trust His purposes for your life. He wants only your good (Ps. 23; Matt. 6:25–34; 2 Cor. 9:8–10).

By the Way, Boss, I'm Having a Baby

Your first impulse when you become pregnant will be to announce the happy news to everyone, especially the co-workers with whom you have a friendship.

Don't. For one thing, the risk of miscarriage is greatest during your first three months. Second, it's wise to keep your immediate superior's confidence by telling him or her first, before your news hits the grapevine.

Think through in advance that conversation with your boss. Plan how you'll answer questions about scheduling doctor's appointments and handling possible emergencies. If you plan to return to work after maternity leave, reassure your employer. But avoid giving a definite date when you plan to go on leave. Early in pregnancy you can't forecast how you'll feel during later months, especially if this is your first child. So just say, "I really haven't decided yet."

Your employer may not be thrilled with your pregnancy. You've been trained for your job, and now you're doing what men often deem "just what women always do." Nevertheless, be straightforward, not apologetic. Keep your discussion and attitude professional and positive. Check out your company's policy on maternity leave and/or the pregnancy conditions of your group health plan. (For example, many companies allow maternity leave, but without pay. You'll want to know that.)

If you're debating whether to return to work after giving birth, use these months of pregnancy as a trial run. Bank your salary and live on your husband's. That will provide you a nest egg for the future as well as a realistic glimpse of how well you'll function on one paycheck.

Not every successful career woman wants to resume her work after delivery. Some are surprised to discover how much they relish caring for their own baby. After years of working with things, they may be anxious to take a break and devote themselves to nurturing and training living beings. Time enough to pick up their careers later on, they reason.

Few women are free to make that decision, however. Mortgage payments and monthly bills continue—and grow. The husband's income may be insufficient. He may judge it unfair for you suddenly to award him the entire financial burden of your life together. Notwithstanding, don't make dollars your only determining factor. Couples who agree on a goal (such as mother being in the home full time) will manage to work out finances and maintain a strong marriage. Sacrifice doesn't depress them, because they share a purpose they consider worthwhile. Such couples usually find that the experience bonds them more strongly than ever.

If and when you return to work, it's worth noting that working mothers can still breast-feed their infants, even when separated all day. Many nursing mothers keep a breast pump at work. They express their milk in the rest room, then store it either in the office refrigerator or in the refrigerated water cooler. The next day, the sitter uses that milk to bottle-feed the baby. (La Leche League, the organization for nursing mothers, can offer helpful advice.)

Rarely may a mother bring her baby along to work and put the infant in a carriage, portable crib, or playpen—although some companies sponsor reliable child care on the premises. For most women, however, it is not an option.

Is There an Ideal Family Size?

T ime was when an only child was routinely linked with terms such as "lonesome" and "spoiled brat." Today there seems to be evidence that an only child who grows up in a secure home actually may be more self-assured and more intellectually advanced. Two children to a family is also a popular choice.

Many parents, however, desire larger families. "I grew up with three brothers and two sisters," says Naomi. "We had no money, but we had a wonderful life. I think that's the best lifestyle on earth for kids—they learn how to get along with other people. All my life I dreamed of having six kids myself. But nowadays, when anyone has more than two or three kids at the most, they're looked on as a curiosity. Besides, Paul says we simply cannot afford more than three. I guess he's right . . . but it's so hard to say good-bye to those laughing children who will never be."

Basic math would seem to show that with growing numbers of childless-by-choice marriages, space becomes available for larger families—without upsetting anyone's equation. So if your family numbers more than four, either now or in the future, don't apologize. Fill your children's basic needs. Give them abundant love and a secure home. Lead them to know Jesus Christ as their Savior from sin and their best Friend. Do that, and you'll supply everything your offspring will need to develop into stable, responsible, emotionally whole adults—whether you have one child or a houseful.

Still, if you're considering enlarging your family, it's wise to make sure neither your partner's nor your own thinking has changed. Here are some thought-starters:

• Do you love and enjoy your present children? (That differs from liking kids in general; some of the most successful and loving parents aren't particularly attuned to other people's youngsters.)

• Are you emotionally ready to commit to the responsibility of caring for another child? (Don't think of two children as just one child doubled. Instead, you have two individuals needing and wanting different things from you, at different times, often in different places. Nor are three children simply 50 percent more than two children. Etc.)

• Can you financially handle the added expense? (Notice that the question is not, Do you have money available in your budget? That answer is always no. Unless you're truly at rock bottom, when your hearts have room, the finances somehow take care of themselves.)

• Is your marriage sound? Does understanding flow between you? Do you share the child-rearing? (Even the best mothers have limits to their energy and endurance.)

• How will you work out child-care arrangements?

• Is there any physical risk involved in another pregnancy?

• Does either of you have any doubts about adding another child to your family?

By the way, money—or the lack of it—has little to do with the success or failure of a family. "Our home was poor in possessions, but we were rich in love!" says Alice. "I'll be forever grateful that we had to make do with what we had. I discovered that there's nothing I can't do if I put my mind to it. I learned to use my ingenuity and my creativity. I wouldn't trade those humble early years for anything in the world!"

The Truths of Past Generations Still Stand

Realize that although we live in a world where change has become the only thing we can count on, the timeless truths of bringing up children stand firm. Parenthood *is* uniquely fulfilling; nothing else quite compares. The challenge is daily and demanding, but the joys are also daily—and abundant. Rearing children together provides a couple with a common purpose, a shared joy.

Those who opt to forego a family often look back on that decision with deep regret. Many who once felt they "had it made" come to the conclusion—years to late—that their life purpose was paltry and pointless. As human beings, we're created to need other people—and we need to be needed. Children fulfill both requirements, at least for the immediate future. Once your responsibility ends and your children have matured into friends, that mutual bond will enrich each of you all your days.

Your children are God's gift to you all their lives—and your gift to the world.

Sons are a heritage from the Lord, children a reward from him. (Ps. 127:3)

He settles the barren woman in her home as a happy mother of children. (Ps. 113:9)

The birth of our children remains the high point of my life. Never before nor since have I felt such overwhelming joy. It was too great to talk about, even with Hank. I just stared at their faces and wept. We've had so many good times, so many moments of pure happiness. Oh sure, it has often been a strain. The women I work with drive sports cars; I drive an old clunker because we have medical bills and orthodontia. But really, I've never minded. They're our children, and we love them with all our hearts—it's that simple. Would I do it over again? You bet your life! (Wife)

The best advice I ever had was to be 100 percent Mommy at home and 100 percent worker on the job—and never to mix them up. That has kept me sane! (Wife)

8

Who Will Care for the Children?

When I went back to work, I was terribly hard on myself for months. I could see that our girls were getting excellent care, but I felt I was letting them down because I wasn't there. Finally it hit me: Even full-time mothers don't spend every waking minute stimulating their children. That seems pretty obvious now, but it was a breakthrough at the time. I felt as if the weight of the world fell off me that day.

—Mother

This life-style is not easy! Seems when I have a frantic day at the office, that's the night my three-year-old whines all evening and the baby wakes several times during the night. It's like being hit with a double whammy—and it happens too often!

—Mother

I don't like leaving Alexander home alone after school. After all, he's only nine. But he fusses that he's too old for a sitter . . . and he is very responsible. I pray a lot!

—Mother

What do children of the dual-career couple need, beyond basic care and feeding?

- Unqualified love and acceptance
- A perception that their family is stable
- As few changes as possible in persons providing care
- Emotional stability in the care giver
- Consistency in values and discipline between parents themselves and between parents and care giver(s)
- A home atmosphere (and day-care surroundings) that encourages them to be individuals
- One-to-one time (regularly) with each parent
- The immovable foundation of faith in Jesus Christ as Redeemer, undergirding all of life

Obviously, this is an ideal list. Few, if any, families anywhere, anytime, achieve all of these—but the two essentials for well-balanced children are the first and the last.

Don't overlook the importance of harmony between yourselves and your care giver, either. When a child spends daytimes operating under one value system and nights and weekends under another, emotional damage could result. As for the rest of the list, do the best you can. Comfort yourself with this unshakable truth: Children who know absolutely that they're loved can handle the ups and downs of life and emerge emotionally secure.

The Lady of the House Is a Man

Some parents of young children, uneasy about leaving their offspring in the care of others, are trying a new tack. Enter Daddy, the house-husband. Actually, some men make better mothers than their wives. The father may have a more nurturing temperament, may be more patient, more relaxed. So the arrangement may be just right for all concerned.

After William was born, Brad took over his care, and Monica returned to work. "I think I'm pretty mellow," says Brad. "Takes a lot to make me blow my stack. Monica is a born pusher, making her mark in finance. Besides, she earns three times what my little business brought in, so this was a logical solution."

"In the early months, Brad was lots more comfortable with William than I was," Monica admits. "He saw himself as the expert—always telling me what William liked and how I should hold my son. Kind of resented that at first, until I realized it was simply because Brad was around all day. Once I came to terms with that, I was okay.

"I get home from a long commute, so I snatch time with William whenever I can," she continues. "That's more important to all of us than keeping a strict schedule. So far, William seems pretty flexible. Weekends I take over. But Brad and William have something special between them. I envy that, even though I'm glad for their closeness. And I have to admit that sometimes I feel like excess baggage. Brad does such a super job all by himself."

This new arrangement solves many logistical problems for the working mother, but it may create new problems within the marriage relationship. For example, the husband without a paycheck lacks that traditional, tangible proof of worth, so his self-image may suffer. The wife, although receiving monetary reinforcement, inevitably feels somewhat displaced in the usual mother-child relationship. Moving in completely different worlds, the couple may find less to talk about than before. Embarking on this life-style will take both partners outside their "comfort zones" (customary role expectations). Change always knocks away a few props, so for a while the couple will feel their way, developing their own style.

Friends and family may not be supportive. The curious will speculate, some will criticize—and a few people will only question the husband's masculinity. The wife, too, may be taunted about her husband, the wimp. Add to that the internal strains already mentioned, and either or both may begin to lash out at each other.

"Brad has been so good, so loving," says Monica. "Yet I find myself nagging at him, just like the old TV sitcom husband who gets impatient with his stay-at-home wife. It's always something dumb, like kidding him about the new love handles around his waist, or asking why he doesn't read the business section so that he knows what goes on in my world. I truly am glad we can do this, but I guess we're still adjusting. Even after more than a year, it still feels a bit strange."

Some people wonder whether children raised more by the father than the mother will lack clear definition between male and female. That's not a problem when both parents are secure in their own identity. Children almost always model after the parent of the same sex, regardless of who does what within the family.

Since the wife typically earns less than her husband, relatively few couples can afford this life-style. As wages become more equal—and as more people realize that self-identity and worth come from within, not from gender-dictated roles—acceptance will grow. After all, both wife and husband retain their position in the Lord, no matter whose name the family paycheck bears.

There are some definite pluses. The working mother enjoys the peace of mind that comes from knowing that her child is being cared for by the person she loves and trusts implicitly. The house-husband moves out of the father-observer role into that of primary care giver, thus building a relationship impossible to achieve were he functioning as an "old-fashioned father." And don't overlook benefits to the child, who basks in parental love full time.

You can't take yourselves too seriously if you're to make this arrangement work. You also need agreement of purpose, willingness to compromise, and a ready sense of humor to ease you over the bumps. Make it your mission to build each other up at every turn, verbally and in action. That mutual reinforcement will enable each to give up bits of your "personal territory" without feeling diminished. And don't forget to nurture your love relationship as well, in word and deed, so that your couple foundation remains firm.

F *Wanted: A Loving Mother Substitute*

or most working mothers, finding outside child care remains their biggest continuing concern—that and resolving distress over leaving their children every day.

Once upon a time the woman who worked could count on her children's grandmother or perhaps a maiden aunt to serve as a substitute mother. The second choice was another mother, preferably with similar-age children—and there were usually several to choose from right in her own neighborhood. These women, busy raising their own youngsters, hesitated only slightly before taking on one or two more.

Today's situation bears little resemblance to that uncomplicated picture. Grandma, if not employed herself, either lives too far away or relishes her own freedom after years of child-rearing. Starting over with diapers and Pablum and crayon-on-the-walls lacks appeal. Any "maiden aunts" have their own careers, and few at-home homemakers populate our neighborhoods.

Although many mothers would prefer having someone come into their homes each day to provide child care, cost usually eliminates that option. That leaves group care, either with an individual or at a day-care center. And it entails depositing offspring on the way to work. Just coordinating the morning's comings and goings can be a marvel of logistics.

"Every morning I deal with a dozen complications before I ever arrive at work," says Ann. "I have to drop off the baby and all his gear at the baby-sitter's. Todd, our four-year-old, attends preschool across town. Mason is in second grade and rides the school bus, which comes after I leave. So I have to shoo him out the door to the neighbor's before I take off. After school, when my neighbor is at work, I have an older lady from church stay 'til I get home. Sometimes she calls in sick, and then I have to telephone around for a last-minute replacement. So my afternoons can get difficult, too.

"Most of the time it's your normal hectic routine, but once in a while the whole thing falls apart. Todd will wake up with a fever and there goes the day care—or Mason has a tummy ache. A couple of months ago, my long-time baby-sitter announced out of the blue her plan to move within two weeks. Talk about panic! So I never know when I get up what the day will bring. I try to take it 24 hours at a time—that's all I can manage. If nothing else, I'm learning to handle frustration."

Often Dad takes over chauffeur duty, which lessens that morning stress for Mom. But working mothers dread those phone calls by dawn's early light. They know by experience that it likely means they must launch a search to uncover a last-minute replacement or miss a day's pay. To say that this is a constant stressor is grossly to underestimate the strain.

A child running a fever—or one who has diarrhea or is vomiting—is a worry for any mother but a disaster for a working mom. Neither individual care givers nor licensed care centers want sick children. Substitutes on your list find excuses when your child is ill. Then there are school holidays and snow days and broken-furnace days. You hear on the early news that school will be closed today and groan. Now you have one or more school-agers with nowhere to go. And your adversary, the clock, moves on relentlessly.

So what's a mother to do?

For your own peace of mind, have a backup system in place—before you need it. Perhaps a neighbor would care for your ill child in an emergency. A relative or fellow church member might agree to be available for last-minute calls. Talk with several persons individually if you can. If they don't know your child well, be sure they have a chance to get acquainted and that they relate well with each other. Talk through expectations—your own and those of the prospective pinch hitter. Mutually agree on compensation. In other words, cover all the bases ahead of time. It might also be a good idea to write down the terms and guidelines you have agreed on and to mail a copy to these persons so that none of you has surprises later on.

Check on your own and your husband's employer policy concerning employee sick days, personal time days per year, etc., and maintain a running total of what you've used so far. File this information together with phone numbers of those willing substitutes. Keep this file (or your master list) in a handy place, ready to grab in emergencies. Then when you are rushing to organize your morning and you have a last-minute complication (is there any other kind?), you can deal with it more calmly.

Day-Care Alternatives

Many books do a good job of delineating the factors involved in choosing trustworthy day care. Briefly, begin by considering the obvious first candidate: Grandma. Although this sounds like an ideal arrangement, it may have several drawbacks. For one thing, mothers/mothers-in-law sometimes develop hurt feelings if you suggest that she make changes. After all, she raised you (or your husband) and you turned out okay, didn't you? So you, the working mother, bite your tongue because you must maintain a good relationship at all costs.

Before you finalize that arrangement, ask yourself:
- Will Grandma remember that this is *our* child?
- Is she in good health, with ample energy?
- Are her values and faith similar to ours?
- Does she *want* to baby-sit?
- Am I comfortable talking with her about feelings?

If the answer to one or more of those questions is no, reconsider this proposition carefully.

By the way, free child-care doesn't exist. If a relative accepts the responsibility without charge, you become "beholden." You can't upset Grandma, after all, who has been so generous—even if you feel frustrated at the way she deals with your child. So insist on giving at least a small weekly salary—"for pocket money." Psychologically, you'll feel entitled to be a bit more assertive and to ask for changes you feel are necessary.

A younger mother with children of similar ages—and compatibility with your own—may be less disquieting in the long run. If you don't know such a person, ask other working mothers for recommendations. Depending on the laws of your state and the number of children she cares for, this person may or may not be licensed. If you know her, it probably won't make any difference to you.

Look for a woman you can respect—one who provides child care for valid reasons. For example, she may want to remain home with her own child. Or her children may be in school, and she misses caring for babies/toddlers. Although she is in the business to earn money, should you discern that money seems to be her only motivation, walk the other way.

Your church newsletter or bulletin could be a good instrument for locating prospective care givers. Instead of heading your notice "Baby-Sitter Needed," why not title it "Substitute Mom/Grandma Needed"? Respondents to such a notice will likely be just that type—and isn't that what you really desire?

Christian parents able to leave their children in the care of other trusted, loving Christians are truly blessed. Knowing that the beliefs and values of the care giver harmonize with their own affords a sense of peace. Best of all, they needn't fear that their children will be exploited, assaulted, or ill-treated.

Check Thoroughly Before You Choose

In every instance, use your common sense and do as much preliminary checking as possible. Nevertheless, trust your instincts, too. For example, you may find a person who appears superbly qualified, yet you're vaguely uneasy around her. Or a woman may seem capable, but you really don't like her very much. Perhaps your child seems to have an unfounded wariness. No matter how convenient or economical the arrangement, remember that you're setting yourself up for emotional turmoil at the very least. Ask God to guide you—to enlighten the eyes of your minds so you can choose wisely. Then if you feel any inner hesitation, think twice. That may be God's early warning system through the Holy Spirit.

Once you've located a prospect, request references from other parents and *check them out,* even if this person is a friend-of-a-friend. When interviewing, be ready with well-defined questions. Inquire about her values, her life history, her health, etc. Ask her opinions on methods of discipline. Does she seem sensitive and willing to accept children's individual levels of development? How much television (and what programs) are children allowed to watch? Be explicit about what you expect—and will not tolerate—in particular areas such as punishment methods, snacks, sugar, "baby talk," smoking around your child, etc. Get her views on cuddling, recreation, toilet training, and scheduling (must all children take naps at the same time, or does she adapt to differing ages and stages?).

Many of the same guidelines apply for both individual care givers and day-care facilities.

Routinely inquire what children do on a typical day. If you get a vague answer, suspect that they mostly watch TV. (One woman bought VCR tapes of *Star Wars* and *Superman,* saying, "The kids love these! They watch them every day and never get tired. Keeps them off my hands and quiet for hours.")

Check for cleanliness, of course. Most of us have no qualms about inspecting a public facility but shrink from asking to see the bathroom(s) and kitchen in an individual's home. Don't be embarrassed; you have the right—and the obligation.

Where do children play during inclement weather?

Where do they rest/take naps?

Is there space where children can be alone for a while if they choose?

Do you have a feeling of space—of good light and air? Or is the children's indoor play area cramped and dark?

Is there an outdoor play area? Is it satisfactory and safe?

Is the yard securely fenced and the gate firmly latched?

Are there smoke alarms?

You needn't feel awkward about such in-depth inquiry and inspection. Time spent getting answers beforehand can spare you a lot of frustration later. As a concerned parent, it's your right—and your duty—to be meticulous in choosing. This woman is applying to you for a paid position. Unavoidably, she'll influence your child, for they'll spend every day of your workweek together. You want that impact to be for your child's lifelong benefit.

Be a Careful Observer

If the prospective sitter cares for other children, try to spend some time observing. Be there in the morning to watch the children's moods as they arrive. Drop in unannounced and spend an hour or so. Do the youngsters seem happy or bored? How does she handle squabbles? What activities does she provide? Does she furnish lunch? If so, what does she serve? Are toddlers allowed to feed themselves? How does she react when children are fretful or unhappy? Inquire, too, how long these particular children have been in her care. In other words, does she have frequent turnover? If she does, find out why.

As a final step, arrange for your child to be with the prospective care giver(s). Observe the two of them together, from within the room and without. Try to pick up the "chemistry" between them. When she holds your baby, does she seem relaxed and confident or tense and awkward? Is she gentle or rough? If you sense good rapport and decide to hire her, try to get a tentative time commitment. How long does she plan to be in business? Your purpose is stability, because its presence (or absence) could affect your child's ability to form lasting relationships, both now and in the future.

Once you've hired a care giver, drop in without warning a time or two. It will ease your mind indescribably when you feel that you know—and approve—what's going on in your child's day. When you deliver and pick up your child, don't just dash in and hurry out. Allow time to talk and to build a relationship. Even with a close relative, you need to discuss informally how things are going and/or resolve any differences.

Help your substitute—your partner—to understand your child. For instance, once in a while your child will start the day sad or crotchety because of a home experience. Be sure to advise the care giver why. Tell her that Jason's puppy was run over, that Alison just had a DPT shot, that Joseph didn't sleep well last night. Equipped with your insight, she can provide more sensitive care.

P *Relax—Your Child Knows Who You Are*

erhaps you're troubled and torn because someone else spends 40-plus hours per week with your beloved offspring. You fear being displaced in your child's heart. Instead of fretting, be constructive. Bend your efforts toward nurturing a close, warm relationship with your children that is the foundation of their life. Communicate your love so surely that your child basks in its security. Then Mary Poppins herself could not replace you in your child's affections or allegiance.

Nevertheless, leaving behind your much-loved child five days a week can be distressing. Guilt moves in to grab a free ride and chip away at your confidence. In fact, some mothers respond by trying to make up for the hours of separation by talking fast, playing hard, holding their babies every minute.

Relax. Your child knows that you are the mother. Out of sight is not out of mind, even between a very young child and its mother. Put away the guilt and just be loving. Be at ease, and your child will be, too. Yours remains the primary relationship, yours the greater influence. Rest assured, your children will likely grow up strong and stable, even if the care giver has minor deficiencies.

B *The Day-Care Center*

oth individuals and larger licensed day-care facilities have advantages—and drawbacks. While an individual typically cares for fewer children, they may be left to their own devices for long periods of time. Licensed centers often provide more intellectual stimulation through group activities, yet there may be little personalized attention. Each child may be counted as a "unit," and a certain number of units produces a certain number of dollars. Some centers are excellent; others are merely parking garages.

Look for a day-care center with a low ratio of children per adult. General recommendations are one adult for every three babies or toddlers, one adult to every four in the two- to three-year-old range, one adult to every eight youngsters over age three. Play groups should be composed of children within a two-year age span. Smaller groups are better than large at any age, even when optimum teacher-child ratios are observed. Maximum play-group sizes: 6 children up to age two, 12 for the twos and threes, 16 for the three- to six-year-old children. Teachers should be trained and experienced. Workers should be reasonably well paid. Do staffers seem content? What's the turnover rate for personnel?

Obviously, you'll seek attractive, clean surroundings. In addition to the points mentioned earlier, there should be one crib per infant; each child should have a mat or a crib in which to nap. Play equipment, indoors and outdoors, should be appropriate and well maintained. Check to see whether current licenses are displayed as well.

Again, spend some time observing. Try to avoid nap time or the end of the day. Rather than watch the group, pick one or two children or one small group. Are the children contented? Do they seem lively or bored? Are they absorbed and interested in what they're doing? Or do they welcome interruptions?

Look for children's drawings posted on the walls. Do teachers move around from one child to another so that all get attention? Note whether babies are played with or left in cribs or playpens to amuse themselves. Find out whether parents are free to come and go. If not, why not?

Try to arrange your schedule so that you can volunteer some time at the preschool or day-care facility. That's your opportunity to get a fix on the atmosphere in which your offspring spends most waking hours. Such exposure will help you evaluate your child's comments from a more informed perspective.

Get in the habit of asking your child, "What did you do today? What kind of games did you play? Show me how to play, too. Can you teach me the songs you've been learning?" etc. If you have trouble drawing out your child, pass out paper and drawing materials. Borrow a technique used by professionals: ask your child to draw pictures of their activities and games they play. Sometimes children can express themselves on paper when they can't/won't in words. Remember, this isn't an interrogation, so keep it light. But such questions, asked often, will afford you a composite view of the care giver's day-to-day operational style.

Once in awhile drop in unexpectedly during the day or pop in for lunch. Avoid returning from work at exactly the same hour each day. Have your husband stop occasionally, too. If distance makes that difficult, a neighbor or relative might do so for you. The surprise element should guarantee a more accurate gauge of normal daytime activities and interaction than would be possible by taking stock when the care giver is prepared for your appearance.

Try to meet parents of other children in the group and exchange phone numbers. Then you can compare opinions occasionally. In case your child communicates something that leaves you puzzled or uneasy, you'll have someone to call. Often, just hearing another viewpoint (or even the same story verified) will set your mind at rest.

Confronting the Unspeakable

Horror stories concerning child-care providers continue to surface. Some are individuals, some are staff members of larger, even well-respected, group-care centers. Parents are understandably shattered to discovered that they'd entrusted their children to people who sexually abused/exploited them. (Remember that most child molestation is done by a family member or friend—someone the child is used to seeing around home—not by strangers or those outside the family circle.)

Sexual abuse is an ugly fact of life decent people would rather not think about. Besides, as a working mother you *must* have a substitute care giver. So as each loathsome incident makes the news, you—and working mothers all over the country—may process an unspeakable thought: Perhaps my child is in such an atmosphere. Might I be paying someone to harm my child? Obviously, there are decent, loving parents who've been appalled to discover just such a nightmare in their lives. Most of the time we blot that hideous possibility from our minds, relegating such human depravity to "somewhere else"—anywhere but in our own community.

That reaction may lull your fright, but it does nothing to protect your child. Nor does it help to become consumed by fear and suspicious of everyone. So deal with the truth. Sexual abuse is real, even though the chances of your own child being molested are statistically small. Sexual molestation occurs in home-care as well as in large day-care centers, in small towns as well as in populous urban areas. Intelligence, poise, and personal appearance are not reliable indicators of a person's morals. You've probably noticed news photos of accused sex offenders who appeared to be pleasant-looking, grandparent-type individuals. As usual, evil can disguise itself as attractive and harmless.

So take precautions. In addition to all the careful investigation you do, prepare your children. Teach them the proper terminology for genitals. Repeatedly reinforce the concept: "Your body belongs just to you. It's okay when people who love you, like Daddy and me and Grandma and Grandpa, hug you and hold you on our laps. And sometimes grown-ups may help you when you use the toilet or when you're sick. But they're not allowed to touch you here or here [point toward the genital and rectal areas] when you're away from us. If somebody tries, you just tell them, 'Please don't touch me there; that part of me is private.'

"Even if they tell you, 'It's okay; your mommy said we could play this new game,' you say no! If anyone ever touches you that way, you come and tell me right away. *I will always believe you!* And I'll *always* look out for you."

If your children ever complain of pain, *pay attention!* Small ones may not be able to tell you, but they can show you. ("Put your hand where it hurts, Honey. Tell me what made it start hurting.")

That's another reason why it's vital that you and your children establish an early, unshakable bond of mutual trust and honesty. Both of you need the absolute confidence that each will tell the truth—without fail. That allows your child courage to confide in you, even if threatened or warned not to talk. And you'll be assured that your child isn't dealing in fantasy.

If the worst were to happen, and you discovered that your child has been mistreated, comfort yourself with this: Youngsters who are secure in the love of their parents seem remarkably able to come through even such trauma with few lasting effects.

Design a Family Alert System

By the way, think ahead to possible scenarios that might involve someone stopping by "in your place" and removing your child from either day-care or grade-school premises. Begin with the people in charge. Give them a password and insist that they file it with your child's records. You might use your mother's maiden name, your place of marriage, etc.; make it something rather obscure, as banks often do.

Make it very plain that when you authorize another person to transport your child (such as in a car pool), you will notify the supervisor in advance. In addition, any individual who might appear unannounced will have been informed of the password. Without that password, they're *not* to release your child into the custody of *anyone,* even if that person claims to be the child's grandmother. Speak with the individual teacher/ care giver as well and go through the same points.

Obviously, such an arrangement will complicate your life if you forget to forewarn someone who's running your errands. Measured against your peace of mind and your child's safety, however, any inconvenience fades.

Next, talk with your children. Very young children can't be trusted to remember a password. Tell them, however, that they're not to get in the car with anyone unless they've gotten permission from the grown-ups in charge—or from you or your husband, if at home. For older children, agree on a password. Aim for something different than the one given the day-care/ school personnel. It might be a family joke, a nonsense rhyme, or even something from daily life: "Tell me what kind of shampoo I used this morning. What did I want for my birthday dinner? What did I call Grandma when I was two?" etc. Again, choose something that anyone outside the immediate family would be unlikely to guess or to pick up by overhearing casual conversation.

Be honest with your child about the need for precautions, but lighten any sense of foreboding by comparing your family password arrangement to membership in a secret society. Most youngsters like that concept.

Methods don't matter. The point is to help both you and your children feel more secure. Warning children not to get into a car with a stranger has always been basic common sense. Today children see pictures of missing children printed on cartons and bags and telecast between programs. Some are haunted by the thought: "What if someone came and told me my folks said to come with him? How would I know he was telling the truth?" Parents wonder the same thing. So design your own signal system—and emphasize that this is private, not to be shared with others.

In brief, do all that you can to be wary and wise, but don't lose your perspective. You don't want to live in perpetual suspicion or make your child fearful—just cautious.

When all is said and done, though, you must face facts: You can't constantly and personally monitor the situation. So it's well to appropriate your privilege as a Christian mother. Daily commend your child to God's care and protection. Turn your attention to the Bible and read some of God's pledges of protection and peace: Ps. 9:9-10; 28:6–7; 32:7; 34:7; 55:22; 56:3–4; 91; 121; Prov. 3:6, 23–24; Is. 26:3; Matt. 10:29–31; John 14:27; Rom. 5:1; Phil. 4:7; Col. 3:15. Share these promises with your children. Together, memorize the verses that you find particularly reassuring and make them your daily watchwords. Decide that as parents and children you will face reality—but you will dwell in God's protection and constant care rather than in the evening news. When fear raises its ugly head again, confess it to your heavenly Father and accept His gift—the peace that passes all understanding.

Each morning, before you leave the house or as you part company for the day, verbally commit your youngsters to God's safekeeping. One or two sentences are all it takes. Send your youngsters off with the precious reminder ringing in their ears: Almighty God is watching over them!

Latchkey Kids

*T*here comes a time in every child's life when he or she announces, "I'm too old to have a sitter! Why can't I come home after school and take care of myself?"

In communities all across the country, care facilities are geared entirely for the young child. Grade-schoolers often have nowhere to go except with each other. A few cities have instituted such after-school programs through their park and/or school systems; so have YMCAs and YWCAs in scattered locations. Yet literally millions of school-age youngsters come home every afternoon to an empty house or apartment.

There seems to be general agreement that after the age of 10 (and some think from the age of 7 or 8), most children are well able to care for themselves. However, whether the practice is damaging to the child remains open to debate. Much depends on how mature you perceive your own children to be. Give them a fair trial at the beginning. Talk with them about why they're assuming responsibility for themselves.

You'll probably establish strict guidelines for when children are home alone. Although helpful to your parental peace of mind, some authorities suggest that rigid house rules make children feel like prisoners—sometimes frightened prisoners. In any case, be sure that your children are stable and sensible for their age, that your guidelines are clearly communicated, and that your offspring have pledged to abide by them.

Here are some suggestions for house rules:

• Be sure that children have your phone number at work. Promise to be available by telephone; it's scary for children who don't know where to turn. If you're unable to take their calls yourself, find a caring substitute who'll either respond directly or relay the information to you.

136

• Have them call you (or your substitute) as soon as they arrive home so that you know they made it safely.

• Try to enlist a trusted, cooperative neighbor who's usually at home as a resource person. He or she can also relay messages if there's a problem with your home phone.

• Post police and fire department numbers (or your community centralized emergency number) by the telephone. Make sure your children know how to give clear information.

• Roleplay possible situations with your children: a persistent knock on the door, obscene phone calls, missing the school bus, a cut that won't stop bleeding, etc. In the beginning, repeat often enough so that responses become automatic. Then run through your routine periodically thereafter to refresh the memory.

• Inform school personnel that your child will be home alone after school.

• Caution children not to tell anyone (except specified individuals) over the phone or at the door that they're home alone. Rather, they should say, "Mommy can't come to the door right now."

• Instruct them to keep doors locked and never to open them to strangers for any reason.

• Children under the age of 14 shouldn't cook unless you're home, except perhaps with a microwave oven.

• Show your children where to find the first-aid kit (well stocked) and the fire extinguisher. Explain how to use them.

• Set up firm rules on one child hassling another and/or who's in charge. (Whether they abide by this is another story.)

• Don't allow pals or neighborhood kids to come into the house. The potential for trouble increases in direct proportion to the number of youthful occupants.

• Assign regular chores and insist that youngsters do their homework in the afternoon. They'll squabble less and you'll have more opportunity for conversation in the evening.

• Remind them that even when there's no one else at home, they're not alone—that God, who loves them dearly, is with them every minute.

Many latchkey children look forward to their hours alone as a "decompression" time after a long day at school. Even secure youngsters face some hazards, however. They're often lonely. Admonished not to have friends over and not to leave the house, they may feel caged. (And if it's dangerous to open the door, what would happen if someone forced his way in?)

Why Not Be Part of the Solution?

Most working parents would prefer their grade-schoolers to be part of an organized after-school activity—one that is reasonable in cost. And no one knows better that the children of dual-career parents could benefit from responsible, Christian care and supervision. Rather than simply to wish for something, contact other parents like yourself and form a nucleus in your church. Discuss the possibilities of setting up a tuition child care program, either after school only or before school as well.

Present the need logically, along with suggestions for implementation. Be the spark plug. If your own church is small, you might cooperate with a nearby congregation. Most churches find such programs not only self-supporting but profit-making. Most important of all, they offer a clear witness to Christian service in the community.

Don't Ignore the Teens

Teenagers who have the whole house to themselves before and after school are especially at risk. With ample uninterrupted time and no adults to monitor them, there's plenty of opportunity for entertaining friends you don't approve of and indulging in questionable activities. Although parents often expressly forbid their teenagers to invite their peers home without adult supervision—or to be in a home without a grown-up present—that's impossible to enforce when you're at work and they're on their own. That's the prime reason why a teenage girl's own home has become the most common setting for sex between teens, as shown by many surveys. (Certainly a bedroom is more comfortable than the back seat of a car.)

As an answer to several problems, consider involving your high school youth group to work in your church's before- and after-school care program. All ages have similar school schedules. Teenagers usually have some experience in baby-sitting. Endowed with youthful energy, they need a purpose. And they're often remarkably creative. With adult supervision and careful planning, everyone would benefit.

Be Calm, but Stay Alert

*L*ike most employed mothers, you're careful and sincerely well intentioned; you want nothing for your child but loving care and protection. Yet no matter how scrupulous you are, so much remains uncertain that low-level anxiety may remain a constant companion.

Don't lose your balanced perspective, but be realistic. No matter what the age of your child, keep your antennae up to detect warning signs. If your older child suddenly becomes quiet, withdrawn, and/or sullen, do some investigating. Is it adolescence or something more serious? If your younger child starts clinging and whining or develops sleeping difficulties, check it out. It may be "just a stage"—or there could be something more serious behind the behavior.

Your goal is to be relaxed but watchful. Some working parents take the ostrich approach, hoping that if they ignore the signs, the situation will somehow resolve itself. Most likely the complaint will be minor. But if your child is troubled, he or she at least needs extra TLC. If not from you, from whom?

On the other hand, beware of mountain-climbing over molehills. Don't manufacture problems where none exist.

You checked and rechecked until you feel like a private eye. You've not uncovered any red flags. Common sense says, "Forget it." Yet you struggle with a gnawing knot in the pit of your stomach—nothing you can identify, just a lack of peace. Or perhaps the nagging guilt pervades your thoughts, *Is Victoria really mature enough to stay by herself after school? My child may be scarred for life, just because I'm not doing my job.*

You can mire yourself down in the mud if you let such thoughts haunt your days. Take that baggage to the Lord and ask Him to sort out fact from fiction. Pray that His Holy Spirit will impress you unmistakably if there truly is need for concern and will give you wisdom to confront what may need to be faced.

If your conviction lingers—and grows—take action to resolve the situation. Pay the price of peace, even though it may complicate your life. Change care givers. Hire after-school supervision. Perhaps even give up your job, if that seems the only way for now. Your outlook (and probably your health) will improve. And your children will mirror your calmer attitude.

On the other hand, you may find that, after prayer, your doubts and fears seem to subside. Accept that as the Spirit's leading, too, and go in peace.

Although it's too early to tell the long-term effects of leaving the current generation of children in the care of others, at least two points are settled, once and for all:

1. God gave us our children, and we're responsible to Him for their nurturing, their guidance, their care. We do the very best we can. We can do no less.
2. Each day we commit our children to the almighty Creator of heaven and earth, who watches over them every moment. We claim His promises—for our children and for ourselves. That is all we need!

If you make the Most High your dwelling . . .
then no harm will befall you,
no disaster will come near your tent.
For he will command his angels concerning you
to guard you in all your ways;
they will lift you up in their hands,
so that you will not strike your foot against a stone. . . .
"Because he loves me," says the Lord,
"I will rescue him;

I will protect him, for he
 acknowledges my name.
He will call upon me, and I will answer him;
 I will be with him in trouble,
 I will deliver him and honor him."

(Ps. 91:9–11, 14–15)

9
Balancing the Stresses: Your Marriage and Your Job

Perry sometimes says that I'm getting too "bossy" around home. Maybe he's right. After all, I am the boss at work.
   —Wife

My wife's a workaholic. The money is fine, but she brings so little to our marriage lately that I'm afraid it may go down the tubes. I love her, but I can't make it work all by myself.
   —Husband

It's hard to have Christi earning so much more than I do. How can I feel like the head of the family when she pays most of the bills?
   —Husband

I think I have a right to spend what I earn, with no questions asked. It infuriates me that Benjamin even comments, let alone tries to control how I handle my own money!
   —Wife

All those years, killing myself to land this job . . . and now I'm finding that the view from the top isn't so terrific after all.
　　—Wife

My husband actually expects me to give up my job and follow him across the country! But I've invested years building a career with this company. To start all over again would be a terrible waste.
　　—Wife

Kyle is so jealous that he has no perspective at all. I'm just an average-looking woman, but you'd think I was Miss America with male co-workers falling at my feet!
　　—Wife

I just don't have a thing in common with Susan's friends! They're all white-collar professionals, and I'm a plumber. Her friends don't want to hear about the trials of cleaning out a septic tank, and I can't identify with amortization tables. Why can't she give it up?
　　—Husband

People's responses to any given situation are as individual as fingerprints. What one working wife finds exhilarating, another considers depressing. The situation that dismays one woman causes another to assess her options calmly and to act, never breaking stride. That makes it impossible to give exact formulas for dealing with the inevitable stresses inherent in the two-paycheck marriage. One caution remains constant, however: Don't undervalue your marriage relationship and/or take it for granted—which is dangerously easy to do. When one or both partners strive to rise in their careers, their marriage often takes second place. At the end of a typical high-pressure day, each could say, "I gave at the office." And they did—their energy, their concentration, their commitment.

"Of course, our marriage is important to us," says Jane defensively. "But if you want to make your mark on the job, you have to make things happen—and fast. Rick and I both understand that and make allowances for it. Later, when things quiet down, we'll have plenty of time for each other."

That "logical" attitude, which is all too common, falls under the category of "famous last words." Most couples find that "later" keeps getting moved into the future.

The attitude widely considered essential to success in the workplace—independent thinking and assertive behavior—constitutes another hazard to marriage. To strengthen the couple bond, each partner needs a mind-set that says, "What's good for you is good for me; 'we' are more important than either of us individually." (Unfortunately, it's much easier to doff office clothing than to lay aside the workaday frame of mind.)

Making the Transition from Work to Home

Consider the executives who operate every day in an atmosphere where their opinions count, where people fawn over them. Power can be addictive. These power brokers crave intense action—and attention—day and night, for they feel it brings out their best. Such persons, used to giving orders and seeing them carried out without question, often expect that same response at home.

However, when he or she walks through their front door, it's a different world. It's "Would you take out the trash, Dear?" "The baby is cutting a tooth and won't settle down; could you take over?" "I think the transmission is going out in my car; could you carpool and loan me your car for a couple of days?"

After eight hours in the company of the tense and the driven, some movers and shakers come home and settle down in happy relief. Others find the home atmosphere to be small time, perhaps even a bit boring.

Long-standing tradition dictates that an executive (male) needs a supportive mate alongside, preferably a "little woman" type, who will be there when he needs her, emotionally and socially, and who will keep their home running smoothly, even if that only means overseeing paid help.

Picture such a man married to a woman who's also engrossed in a career. He may feel inconvenienced, at the very least. Her time already scheduled, she may be preoccupied with her own concerns. Such a woman likely demands a contributing partner, not just a warm body. Accustomed to a bit of clout herself, she resists dancing to anyone's tune. She is, in fact, the female counterpart to the stereotypical self-centered male.

When both marriage partners are achievers and both want things done their way, living together can deteriorate into a continual contest of wills. Used to holding out for their own position on the job, they dig in their heels more deeply at home and wait for their partner to give up the battle. Few would pronounce this the way to build closeness.

"Laura's not the same woman I married," says Greg. "Her new job is very competitive, and she fights for everything she gets. Trouble is, she brings that attitude home. She argues every point; she's constantly telling me how to shape up. She's preoccupied all the time—even in bed!—with whatever is her latest project. I *am* proud of her, and I love her. But why can't she recognize that I'm not the enemy? I don't want a crisp, efficient supervisor—I get that at work. I want a lover, a listener, a best friend. I think home ought to be where we lick our wounds from the day and prop each other up. I'm perfectly willing to give support . . . but I need that, too!"

Women who set aside their "feminine" qualities on the job sometimes set them aside more or less permanently. Most perceive that as a prerequisite to a successful career. Whether that's a valid assumption remains debatable. Nevertheless, with that mind-set it requires conscious effort to become accommodating and supportive in one's home after a day of "looking out for Number One."

This isn't to imply that the wife is to be the only giver in the relationship. A marriage where one partner always gives and the other always takes is a marriage where one uses the other. Yet many marriages survive because one partner willingly adapts to the other; he or she sublimates personal desires and objectives for the sake of the union. In today's dual-career marriages both husband and wife too often insist on their own rights. That, of course, is contrary to God's design for mutual servanthood to each other and to the Lord.

Anyone who has been married for a while recognizes that the marriage relationship ebbs and flows like the ocean tides. First one spouse most needs nurturing, and the other pours out extra love, extra care, extra support. Then the balance shifts, and their roles reverse. The relationship isn't meant to be fixed and static but moving and adjusting all through life. So flexibility, unselfishness, and an ego that is healthy but not oversized are necessary components to marriage longevity.

The Hazards of Loving Your Work Too Much

Although we all long for work we enjoy, it's no picnic being married to a workaholic. By definition, a workaholic is a person obsessively occupied with work at the expense of normal leisure, human relationships, etc.

Even borderline workaholics, in love with their jobs, find it nearly impossible to turn off their workday concerns. "I think about the business the last thing at night and the first thing in the morning, whether I want to or not," says Eloise. That's a common observation—and few spouses find such behavior thrilling.

Another characteristic of the workaholic is the desire to excel, to perform far above average. Continues Eloise, "I want three things out of life: a happy, supportive, communicative marriage; a couple of healthy, secure, intelligent kids; and success in my field—which to me means the satisfaction of knowing I'm doing a good job. I never worked so hard in my life and yet . . . I have the gut-level conviction that even if I push as hard as I can, I can only do justice to two out of three. That makes me really sad. Yet I can't give up my career! I've been studying and working all my adult life to get where I am right now."

Those comments are echoed by working wives in every section of the employment field. Like Eloise, they simply have too much to do too much of the time. Wise women reach the realistic conclusion that they probably *can't* do superbly in every area every time. If that means that occasionally their effort is Grade B, well, that will have to do. They give themselves permission to relax and accept themselves as human beings. And they keep their focus on what counts most, knowing that if job success comes at the expense of marriage and family, they will have sold out for a mess of pottage.

As a practical beginning, set limits on your involvement with your work. That's how many spouses/parents preserve their sanity—and their marriages. Without that, you can easily become so caught up in your job (and perhaps so charged up by it, particularly if you're a workaholic) that your personal life is barren.

Here are thought-starters to help you spot potential trouble:

- Do you feel a constant sense of time pressure?
- Does your work occupy your mind during many of your off-hours? Is there tension between you and your husband because he resents your job preoccupation? And is that a reasonable claim?
- Do you share the feeling that you've somehow lost touch with each other? Are there tension areas between you—perhaps the same old aggravations day after day?
- Do you ever deliberately avoid spending time with your husband? Do you share leisure time mostly with friends or coworkers instead of your spouse?
- Does life seem dull and gray?
- Do you feel physically better on weekends? (For example, does your headache or indigestion clear up?) Or do you feel worse?

If a couple of these questions hit a nerve, you may be paying too high a price for your success. It could eventually cost you your marriage. So look for solutions. Remember that pretending there are no problems will simply allow them to fester and grow, poisoning other areas of your relationship.

The tug of war between work and family won't end just because you declare its demise. Personal ambition is remarkably tenacious. The first key to victory over the struggle lies in acknowledging the very real gap between what one may hope for and what's actually achievable. To put it another way, you need to reassess your values—reorder your priorities according to reality. The second key—and the one that brings lasting peace—is to realize that as a child of God you don't face this battle alone.

> My flesh and my heart may fail,
>   but God is the strength of my heart
>   and my portion forever.

(Ps. 73:26)

Power Plays

*E*ach husband of a high-earning, high-ranking wife must find his own way of accommodating the arrangement. Some don't cope very well. For example, the formerly agreeable man may become controlling. He aims to demonstrate that he still wields the power in their relationship, so he takes the offensive whenever he can. Once-minor irritants become major.

Or he might choose the opposite approach and withdraw inside himself. He may become depressed, noncommunicative. Some begin to drink too much or eat too much. Conversely, others embark on a physical fitness program or totally change their styles of dress, perhaps to more flamboyant togs.

You could document a dozen variations on this basic theme, but one persistent effect is almost always present. Continual turmoil over roles leads to zero communication. Of course, the couple's relationship suffers.

Popular theory has it that "love conquers all." In fact, however, respect has as much—and probably more—to do with all of a couple's interaction. Respect is the iron reinforcement of the bridge between husband and wife. When respect is lost, either spouse may turn off sexually, not even guessing why—and marriage partners shiver in rejection's chill. That emphasizes again how crucial it is to identify and confront emotions honestly so they can be resolved. Otherwise, those invisible feelings become impenetrable walls.

If you're enmeshed in a similar situation, don't waste time assigning blame. Fight the urge to label your husband as weak or insecure. Instead, look within yourself. Are you perhaps contributing to his feelings? Are you as kind and considerate at home as on the job? Or are you so full of yourself that you don't see his pain, even when it's apparent to the unclouded eye?

Men may feel particularly threatened when their wives achieve in areas once reserved exclusively for men. Such women are often viewed as driven overachievers. That description may be apt. If they weren't far more ambitious and determined than their sisters, these females would choose a less stressful arena in which to earn a living. Predictably, they may carry that attitude home with them.

Avoid the Sugar-Coated Put-Down

It's also true that a wife with job prestige may find it taxing to accept a man who's unemployed, who bounces from job to job, or who hasn't found himself after years of searching. One who makes things happen has little patience with one perceived to lack ambition and/or commitment.

A male caller to a radio advice show discussed his achieving wife—and movingly revealed his own hurt. Perhaps his story is unique. Or perhaps not.

"I'm a potter—a pretty successful one, as potters go. But I don't feel good about myself. In fact, I feel almost like a nonperson.

"My wife's a successful professional. She earns upwards of $70,000 a year.... No, that doesn't threaten me particularly.... Yes, I'm sure my wife loves me—and I love her.... Our sex life? What sex life?

"I'm very proud of my wife's achievements. I just wish she had a little more respect for *my* intelligence. But come to think of it, I guess I haven't been right about much of anything for a very long time. As Katharine says, some people just have a hard time connecting.

"Sure, she's supportive of my art—loves to tell everyone that she's subsidizing her own one-man art commission. So I don't know what I'm complaining about, really."

A wife who specializes in such belittling remarks, either openly or sandwiched in between compliments, reveals her own insecurity. To use a graphic term, by her caustic comments she is emotionally castrating her husband. Her own sense of power comes at the expense of her husband's ego.

Harsh words! However, most of us females possess a quick wit and wickedly sarcastic humor. The same tongue that speaks love so gently can wound like a rapier. (James 3:3–12 aptly describes the tongue's destructive power.)

Before patting yourself on the back and pronouncing yourself blameless, mentally step back and observe yourself for a day or two. Listen intently to your words—and to the nuances as well. (If you're courageous, put on a tape recorder for several hours.) All the while, keep these questions in the back of your mind: Do I like the way I sound? Do my remarks communicate accepting love?

Listen also to discover whether your attitude smacks of superiority, whether you empathize or criticize, whether you affirm your husband and his authority to your children. Most important, have you committed your husband and your marriage to God? Have you asked Him to bring reconciliation and healing to your marriage?

Be brutally honest with yourself. The composite picture of yourself that emerges may shock your self-image. For no matter what your position on the job, if you're not living up to God's image of a servant-wife, you're part of the problem.

That doesn't mean that if your achievement or salary outstrips your husband's, you're expected to apologize or feel guilty. Even though it seems to be the root of the trouble, that disparity isn't the real issue. As usual, attitude is the crux of the matter. If your marriage relationship is deteriorating, fixing blame may be ego-inflating, but it changes nothing. Perhaps your husband *is* a loser. Maybe he does have a lousy outlook on life. And certainly, no matter what his situation, he chooses his responses.

But so do you! And since we humans excel at spotting the specks in our partner's eyes while ignoring the plank in our own (Matt. 7:3–5), you can guess the place to start. Confess your wrong attitude, at least to the Lord. Ask His pardon and His transforming of your heart through the Holy Spirit. Then accept God's forgiveness in Christ—and forgive yourself as well. Ask God to give you eyes that see your husband as God views him—eyes of unconditional love. Lastly, resolve that from this moment on, you are a new person and that you *will* demonstrate your changed nature. Then go forth in God's power and strength—and do it!

L *When You Earn More Than He*

*L*atest statistics indicate that about 1 in 10 working wives now earns more than her husband. That situation represents a shift in the balance of perceived power within the marriage. The wife whose salary surpasses that of her mate will be wise to use extra delicacy and sensitivity in her marriage. In her job she may be used to issuing orders, to passing judgment, etc. But in marriage—coming from either partner—that's the beginning of terminal illness.

Even the wife careful to preserve her mate's self-esteem may find it tough going. Call it male ego if you like, but it has long been an unwritten rule that the wife simply does not hold a more prestigious job than her husband. Nor does she earn more money. Is that up-to-date thinking in the real world? No. But even contemporary couples haven't yet reached that magical kingdom where long-established custom no longer colors their thinking. Reality is one thing. Perception is another.

"Nothing's the same around here since I got that promotion and my big raise," says Anna. "Now Don insists on calling me 'Boss Lady.' When I tell him I don't like that, he says he's kidding, but he's not. If I talk of buying something, he'll say,

'Sure, go ahead. It's *your* money.' If I say I don't have time for a weekend trip, he replies, 'Too bad; I remember what fun we used to have in the old days.'

"Every time I think we have it resolved, he starts all over again. He used to pitch in doing housework without even being asked—all my friends envied me. Now even when I work overtime or on Saturdays, he finds excuses not to help. Or he does such a crummy job that I have to do it over. I don't think I've changed a bit—but he certainly has! And I don't understand why."

Sharing the Wealth

*N*egotiating how the two-income couple will merge—or divide up—the spoils of their mutual stints in the workplace can be tricky. When the subject is money, tempers are likely to flare. Spending decisions can be a hot topic.

Our inherent attitudes toward money have a host of unspoken, often unrecognized connections. The subtle influence spreads like an octopus with tentacles reaching in all directions, invading almost every area of life. And it goes beyond just "love of money" for money's sake.

Perhaps it bears repeating simply because the concept may be unfamiliar to some: Money subconsciously represents power—real or imagined. Both the person with money and the one without would likely argue that, but it slips through in our remarks:

- "They don't have to put up with that—with *their* money!"
- "The rich make their own rules."
- "When Mrs. Lotsabucks talks, everybody listens."
- "They've always had money—never had to lift a finger. They just order other people around. In fact, they run this town."

Think of the terminology we use in discussing money:

- We "give" money; we "take" money.
- The lender (the "have") sets the terms; the would-be borrower (the "have-not") is forced to accept.
- Those of lower income are often termed the "little people."

● People with money are often dubbed "power-brokers," "wheeler-dealers," "power-mongers," "big shots."

Sort Out Your Values

Common sense reminds us that money doesn't automatically award personal worth or happiness—or power, in spite of the terms just listed. Yet bits and pieces of society's values mingle with our own attitudes, conscious and unconscious. So as we hassle over income and spending, we often decipher a message in our partner's remarks that isn't being sent. If your partner seems to be dictating how you can spend your income, you'll rebel—and vice versa.

The audiophile who comes home with a state-of-the-art stereo system will argue in his own defense, "After all, I earn that money myself. I ought to be able to decide how I spend some of it!"

The wife rationalizes her weekly manicure and hair styling appointment as essential. Ignoring her husband's protests, she replies defiantly, "Well, it's *my* money! I have some rights, too. And I should be able to have a treat now and then!"

Say it again: Money is not the problem. Rather, it's the importance—the power—we associate with it. Long ago someone said, "He who pays the piper calls the tune." And for all our sophistication and noble talk, we still adopt the same logic.

"Bill fancies himself the financial wizard at our house." says Wendy. "No matter what I say, he has an answer. It cuts no ice that I earn the money myself. I keep on trying, but Bill gets his way. As I see it, he wins, I lose. But I can't argue with him and his computer printouts."

Wendy and Bill have a problem larger than spending their paychecks. Many couples play out similar dramas. Typically, they put off "money talk" as long as they can, knowing they'll end up on opposite sides of a wide chasm. And building a bridge back takes a long time.

Decide on Goals—Together

If that's a description of you, start by defusing the issue, resolving that you'll be considerate of each other's feelings in this exchange. Take some time to talk about past successes and to concentrate on your oneness. List your previous goals and those you already agree on. Are you making progress? For instance, how much have you invested in Individual Retirement Accounts? What has accrued in your retirement plans at work? How much life insurance coverage do you have? Any savings?

Then take five minutes to brainstorm future goals. Mark those that appeal to each of you, using your initials. Cross out those of no interest to either. Next, both of you rank all remaining goals. Or pick your top three choices and then rank those. Now you have something definite to work with.

Which goals are realistic? Estimate how long it would take to reach them and which could be postponed. Break larger goals into smaller segments. If a desired purchase is too expensive for your budget, perhaps you could buy part of it—or find a cheaper substitute.

By working through these points systematically (and adding some of your own), you avoid a long discussion that goes around in circles. Try to separate emotions from your options so that you remain objective. Be considerate and caring and end your planning session as friends, maybe even as lovers. (Wouldn't that be an improvement!)

Keep Your Priorities Straight

Before you list the rest of your outgo, determine how much of God's money you'll give back to Him. This is your thankoffering—your love response—to what He has given to us: redemption and eternal life through His Son, Jesus; everything that we are; everything that we have. The amount of your love gift is up to you. (Although the Old Testament tithe [Lev. 27:30–32], which probably included taxes, is often held up as a desirable maximum, some Bible scholars believe that it was more likely a minimum.) All through the Bible, however, we're admonished to bring God our "firstfruits," i.e., give to God *first*.

Each man should give what he has decided in his heart to give, not reluctantly or under compulsion, for God loves a cheerful giver. And God is able to make all grace abound to you, so that in all things at all times, having all that you need, you will abound in every good work (2 Cor. 9:7–8).

[Jesus said:] Give, and it will be given to you. A good measure, pressed down, shaken together and running over, will be poured into your lap. For with the measure you use, it will be measured to you. (Luke 6:38)

When as marriage partners you share in this response to God, it's another part of the bond between you. As you grow together in faith, you also grow together in strength.

As for setting up a practical system for handling your paycheck, discuss possible alternatives and find one you can live with. No matter what your aims and methods, remember that money is a tool, meant to enable you to do what you want to do. And you have a choice: Either you will manage your money—or your money will manage you.

It's Your Move—Or Is It?

*T*he dual-career couple faces a difficult decision when one receives an alluring job offer or a transfer to another city or state. Not too long ago it was assumed that when one's marriage and career conflicted, the career automatically took precedence. That's not so certain anymore—for either spouse. These days it may be the wife who receives the enticing offer and the husband who protests. Indeed, partners who face relocation often flatly decline, saying, "I won't consider that move. My mate's career is too well established where we are. If this is an order, I'll have to look elsewhere for employment." (Such sentiments may not land them in the executive suite, but they often lead to a more balanced life with less strain on the marriage.)

The wide range of emotions involved in arriving at a decision makes it a delicate process. The partner being wooed will often be perceived as the "winner." The other partner, who likely has no new position waiting, may say supportingly, "I don't want to stand in your way" and mean it. Nevertheless, when a working wife, for instance, considers giving up what's meaningful in her own life, she may feel a genuine loss—a sense of being merely an appendage who accommodates her spouse.

Objective thinking may be hard to come by. As one aid to a balanced perspective, make two lists—one for your present situation and the other for the new position and/or location. Group the various areas of your lives under three headings:

● *Career* (salary, working conditions, challenge, satisfaction, potential for advancement, etc.)

● *Personal* (neighborhood, friends, relatives, recreational opportunities, church involvement, etc.)

● *Children* (schools, child care, grandparents, friends, etc.)

Now jot down the pluses and minuses in each category. Compare the lists of pros and cons. Consider which partner has the most to gain, which has the most to lose. What would be the effect on your children? your family life? Weigh the significance of one against the other. This simple exercise can clarify your thinking better than continuously talking it over.

With your written list of factors before you, you may decide that the "tremendous opportunity" demands too much sacrifice. That makes it easy to refuse. Conversely, the unenthusiastic partner may realize that the potential benefits make the turmoil of change worthwhile.

Your objective is to arrive at a place of harmony. That doesn't guarantee painless transition, however. For example, the spouse who "trails along" may, after a few moves, pronounce the cost exorbitant.

The Price of Promotion

"My husband's job changes have seriously limited my career," says Billie. "My knowledge and expertise are appreciated, but I'm not paid what I'm worth. Our frequent moves repeatedly put me back at square one. Employers read my résumé and decide either that I'm unreliable or that I'm not likely to stay around. And who can blame them?

"I really have to fight resentment sometimes! But I remind myself of my priorities: (1) Husband; (2) Family; (3) Job. I consciously tell myself—often!—that resentment is self-defeating and hurts me more than anybody else. It could destroy the relationships I care most about. Most of the time I stay on top of it and have a pretty good attitude. But it has *not* been easy!"

The spouse who, like Billie, quits a job to facilitate a mate's transfer is, in most states, disqualified for unemployment compensation. Few companies who transfer John to a new area make any provision for Mary's employment with the same company. Nor do they feel any responsibility to cover costs of acquiring skills usable in the new location. Typically, the spouse without the job offer will be unable to find a position of equal status and salary as the one left behind.

But you may be able to devise some reward for the partner who's giving up a satisfying career to follow along. Think creatively. For example, perhaps John anticipates a significant salary hike. That could afford Mary a long-dreamed-of opportunity to try her hand at another occupation, to open a small business, or to experiment with some sort of free-lance work. She could take a year or so to sharpen present skills or to retrain in another field. The transferred (probably promoted) spouse will already be excited about the move. "Sweeten the pot" for the other partner and help ensure mutual enthusiasm.

Most couples find such transition to be stressful. Even when the job offer results from years of effort, there will be negative as well as positive emotions to work through. Be honest, but avoid being accusatory. It's hardly constructive if Mary says, "*You* make the decision; you're the one with the big raise. Just remember that I'm giving up a lot so that you can have your big break. I hope you appreciate it!" On the other hand, it's perfectly reasonable to say, "I feel sad to give up what I've worked for. I'm uneasy about starting over in an unfamiliar place."

Realize that each rung of the career ladder has a definite price tag attached. Dollars and cents are easy to figure. The intangibles are harder to pinpoint. Entering this new phase of life may or may not be worth it. Whether this transition separates you or bonds you closer than ever depends on what you choose to do with it.

157

"When Karl got promoted, we moved from the city I loved. He got a raise, we moved into a new home, but I sank into a depression that wouldn't quit," says Kay. "After a few months I was drawn to attend a Bible class, and the leader got my attention right away. I don't even remember the text, but I'll never forget the statement that hit me right between the eyes. She said, 'If you're wandering around in a dry, dusty wilderness *of your own making,* open your eyes and look at the countless ways in which God has blessed you. You're in a lush oasis—if you have eyes to see.'

"I felt it was God speaking directly to me through that woman," continues Kay. "That was my turning point. Her remark haunted me and I 'opened my eyes.' Nothing had changed . . . yet everything had changed. Slowly I began to be myself again. And if anyone ever got a lesson in how attitudes affect emotions, it was me."

As with all of life, the stresses in every aspect of the two-career marriage will intensify—or fade—in tandem with our thought processes. And that *is* under our direct control.

Dealing with Jealousy

Another destructive emotion that may arise is jealousy. The employed wife may consider it laughable if her husband fears her eventual involvement with another man. Yet that's a common apprehension. As one husband put it, "Of course I trust my wife. But I know men . . . and they all try it. So yes, I do wonder about that now and then." Similarly, the wife may picture her husband surrounded by dazzling, available female co-workers and unable to resist their charms.

Jealousy needs no factual basis, for it stems mostly from a person's own poor self-image. The mistrustful mate fears that the marriage partner (or even their children) will somehow be lured away by another person who, presumably, is better-looking, has a more winning personality, or has more to offer in some way. Jealousy traps its victims in a whirlpool of fear, suspicion, anxiety, insecurity, inadequacy. Those who struggle with this emotion often criticize and accuse their mates at every turn. This, of course, only drives a wider wedge between them. After all, who wants to be cross-examined continually?

The spouse troubled by jealousy often becomes more possessive, more domineering. In effect, that person is saying, "Prove your love by giving me all your attention, all your loyalty." If the anxious spouse is also experiencing personal insecurity from job loss, health problems, etc., this controlling behavior will probably intensify.

(We're talking here about occasional, fleeting episodes during which a marriage partner displays a level of jealousy that affects the couple's relationship only on the surface. There are, of course, more serious manifestations: continuous jealousy, actual fear on the part of the accused, physical abuse. These behaviors signal a need for professional counseling; go for help at once!)

Filling Emotional Needs

Emotionally, every human being yearns for encouragement and support. We all function better when we're affirmed. If we find our emotional sustenance at home, great! Some don't—and drift into an emotional dependence with a co-worker. Eventually such a relationship may develop into an affair. But the hunger to be nurtured is stronger and more compelling than the desire for sex. An emotionally nourishing marriage relationship remains the most dependable marriage insurance.

Put your efforts into strengthening your bond and confirming your spouse's importance to you. For example, considerate behavior tangibly demonstrates your love and commitment. A simple telephone call explaining that you'll be held up at work can spare you both a lot of heartache. (Then your husband will know that it's work, not your Mr. Wonderful co-worker, that's keeping you away from home.)

Be alert and sensitive to your husband's feelings, even though his anxiety is groundless. Avoid putting yourself into situations that could be misconstrued. If you feel that your spouse is edgy, initiate a frank discussion. Offer you support (again). Reaffirm your commitment to your marriage and restate your love.

Although stressful, dealing with and resolving jealousy can be a growing time for you both. Be creative as you look for ways to reinforce your bond. If you haven't before, pray for your partner—and for yourself. Pray aloud together, if you're comfortable with that—it can weld you together. Guard your own heart and practice forgiveness. Turn again to Scripture for words to live by.

> No temptation has seized you except what is common to man. And God is faithful; he will not let you be tempted beyond what you can bear. But when you are tempted, he will also provide a way out so that you can stand up under it. (1 Cor. 10:13)

> Be completely humble and gentle; be patient, bearing with one another in love. . . . Get rid of all bitterness, rage and anger. . . . Be kind and compassionate to one another, forgiving each other, just as in Christ God forgave you. (Eph. 4:2, 31–32)

Friends: Yours, Mine, and Ours

*B*y definition, friends are people who have something in common—who perhaps share similar interests, life-styles, or careers. Inevitably, each marriage partner will develop personal friendships with co-workers. That can enrich your life or prove to be a problem. Melding the two groups, merging the people from your two worlds, may work—or it may not.

"We either get together with Brett's friends or with mine," says Elda, "but never at the same time."

"Curtis and I each spend time with our own friends," says Sally. "As a couple, we have other friends. Somehow, that works better for us."

Individual friendships pose no threat to a good marriage—unless you choose to consider them a menace. In fact, the diversity among friends enriches us as individuals and we, in turn, bring that richness to our marriage. Yet it's restful to move within a circle of friends and acquaintances who truly understand your own daily challenges. So you may find yourselves gravitating toward others living the two-paycheck lifestyle.

Other dual-career couples listen to your gripes without moralizing—and then feel free to complain a bit to you. They also empathize when you get in a bind; they've been there themselves. Together you sift through the complexities of managing your lives. Such sharing helps to develop a connection that otherwise might not exist.

One caution: as you talk over your common challenges, don't allow your time together to become "garbage-dumping" sessions. Concentrate, instead, on helping each other to find solutions. Bear each other's burdens (Gal. 6:2). Dare each other to grow. Most of all, encourage and support each other.

Practice Preventive Maintenance

The same tactics are useful in marriage, only more so. Just as you take your auto in for a regular tune-up, you need to schedule time regularly to examine your marriage for knocks in the motor. Both you and your husband need to ask yourselves, What's the emotional tab for my career? How does my job involvement affect my marriage? Am I shortchanging my relationship with my spouse?

In areas of conflict, look for the easy remedies first. For instance, a couple may have an every-morning hassle as they hurriedly get ready for work. Both want to use the hair dryer at the same time. Sounds absurd, doesn't it? Solution: buy a second hair dryer. Yet we obtuse human beings often spend months, even years, silently fuming over such small irritations rather than using basic common sense.

Those silly, easy-to-solve problems, however, often go unresolved because they divert attention from deeper problems. Take an honest look within. The two of you may be experts at "stonewalling"—tucking your emotions away in secret hiding places. You know how to bury them deep, smooth over the surface, and plant a fixed smile on each face. But concealed resentments smolder—and one day inevitably explode.

So defuse them by confronting your honest emotions. Face your own contribution. It always takes two, even if one partner just accommodates the other's idiosyncracies. Set pride aside and confess your own responsibility to your partner. Talk it through, using active listening techniques. ("I feel . . . When I hear that, I feel angry . . . It sounds as if you'd like . . . " etc.) By the way, don't equate such purposeful conversation with the endless, intellectual discussions of problems practiced by some couples. You can put the problem under the microscope and examine it from every angle yet remain immobile. Your goal, however, is to deal with it and move on.

Tenderness and sensitivity are mandatory, even though there will likely be some hurtful remarks. Frequently remind yourself—and each other—that you're two lovers resolved to regain some of the early magic, not adversaries out to prove who's "right." Turn up the hearing aid of your love and really listen. Uncover the true stickler(s) in your relationship. As an example, the husband who complains that dinner is "always" late or who blows up over trifles may really be disclosing, "I don't feel important any more. I need your love and attention." The wife who grumbles because "nobody ever helps around here," or who clams up, may be saying, "I feel as if no one cares that I'm tired; I need to know that I'm loved."

Hold hands while you talk, even if it feels phony. (Then you can't avoid touching and looking into each other's eyes; both help thaw the ice.) Keep the process going until each feels understood. Don't settle for anything less, even if it requires several long, painful sessions together. The treasure you'll rediscover by such perseverance is worth every bit of exhausting effort.

Learn to cultivate a sense of oneness by consciously thinking "we"—by deliberately scheduling shared activities as well as "do nothing" time together. Mentally shift gears when you enter your home each evening. Beware of bringing home accumulated gripes and dumping them on each other. Leave your compelling ambition and position at work and become a partner—a servant—within your marriage.

And don't take yourself too seriously. You may be a driver type on the job. Or you may feel like a mindless robot, going through your prescribed routine, one dull day following another. Either way, you've probably numbed your funny bone. Humor and a lighthearted outlook are habits you can develop. (After all, you developed your present attitude, didn't you?)

Practice laughing at yourselves; deliberately collect anecdotes to share. Adopt a confident attitude: of course you can make your marriage more satisfying! You needn't abandon your career plans to do it, either—maybe just slow down your timetable(s). For marriage, like any living thing, needs regular care and feeding—and time to grow. It always has. It always will.

Seek Help from a Pro

What if you never reach that point on your own? What if the gulf between you keeps growing wider? Run, do not walk, to a reliable marriage counselor, preferably a Christian so you'll agree on basic values. Your pastor may be qualified or could refer you to a caring, competent professional.

Countless Christian couples would testify that professional counseling saved their marriages. Even better, it brought them new joy and deeper love because at last they understood and accepted each other. So don't let embarrassment hold you back. Your pastor won't think less of you; he's heard it all before. Intelligent friends and family will be pleased that you value your marriage enough to take action and work together on your relationship. (Besides, which would you rather do—maintain a faultless image or restore your marriage?)

Unfortunately, too often couples seek counseling only as a last, desperate measure. By that time one or the other may have withdrawn, erecting an impregnable wall around their emotions. Deep, long-held pain forges a determination not to dig around in it and be hurt again. When that happens, restoring communication becomes much more difficult.

As Christians, however, we know it's never too late, for we see with different eyes. We worship the God of renewal, who is the wellspring of love.

Forget the former things
  do not dwell on the past.
See, I am doing a new thing!
  Now it springs up; do you not
    perceive it?

Is. 43:18–19

(Surely the God who parted the Red Sea for the Israelites can repair a marriage!)

> Dear friends, let us love one another, for love comes from God. . . . We love because he first loved us. (1 John 4:7, 19)

In light of this last passage, it's apparent that love is more than a warm, melting sensation deep inside—more than the all's-right-with-the-world outlook we experienced during our first big crush. Rather, we decide to love—daily. We also choose—or don't choose—forgiveness and patience.

> As God's chosen people, holy and dearly loved, clothe yourselves with compassion, kindness, humility, gentleness and patience. Bear with each other and forgive whatever grievances you may have against one another. Forgive as the Lord forgave you. And over all these virtues put on love, which binds them all together in perfect unity. Let the peace of Christ rule in your hearts, since as members of one body you were called to peace. (Col. 3:12–15)

Maintaining the Balance

*T*he challenge faced by women who lead two lives, one on the job and one in the home, is more than keeping up with the demands. And the challenge goes deeper than presenting a professional image while maintaining the home front as well. The real challenge is to hold your own in the workday world—which requires a large measure of toughness and assertiveness—and then to leave that person behind at quitting time. Being tough and assertive can be useful and necessary in the marketplace, but it's counterproductive in marriage.

Right now you may be carrying the biggest load of your life, emotionally and physically. Most wives agree, however, that when their marriages are close and warm and nurturing, enjoyment (of everything) goes up and stress (in every department) goes down. Conversely, during rocky periods in the relationship, pleasures pale and the sense of struggle multiplies. So investing extra effort to nourish your marriage returns bountiful benefits. All of life will look and feel better because of it.

To stay sane, don't expect perfection, either from your partner or yourself. And don't take yourself too seriously—hang loose. Learn to laugh. Take time for yourselves—you need it! (Husband)

The bottom line of all my life is my marriage. No matter what I attain or accomplish elsewhere, if I neglect our relationship or feed it only stale crumbs of myself, it will starve. And then I'll have lost the world! (Wife)

10
You Can Make It Work!

*The most important thing—and the hardest to carry off—
is to make sure that our relationship doesn't get lost in
the demands of our jobs and our young children.
Evenings we just manage to make it through 'til the kids
are finally in bed. Then we crash! Spend our weekends
catching up—or trying to. Still, I think we're solid . . .
we're making it work.*
—Wife

*Nobody ever told us it would be easy with both of us
working. But I thought after a while we'd have the kinks
out of our system.*
—Wife

Sometimes I have no energy left to be loving!
—Wife

*All in all, I like our life-style. I don't really want a stay-
at-home wife. I think our kids are well adjusted and our
relationship is good. What more could we ask?*
—Husband

Most working couples admit to a constant feeling of time
pressure. Always it comes down to juggling what's important

against what's simply necessary. For example, it's vital that you get adequate rest or your health will eventually suffer (not to mention your efficiency, concentration, and temperament). But it may seem more important to catch up on the ironing. So management of time is really management of ourselves.

"I've finally comes to grips with the fact that I will never be caught up," says Liza. "I don't like it a bit! But I'm learning, s-l-o-w-l-y, to handle it and not panic."

If you're pushed for time, avoid saying yes too easily. Make a firm rule that you won't add a new commitment without dropping an old one. Yes, the wide world of opportunity beckons. However, the 24-hour day is an unchangeable fact; each additional involvement inevitably translates into more pressure. Life consists of choices, they say, and this is one of the more difficult ones. Treat your time as the precious commodity it is—don't squander it on nonessentials.

Plan Ahead

To keep track of activities, use a calendar with write-in space at home. You and your husband will also need one where you'll list all work commitments and social events. Keep a "week ahead" calendar, too, on which you list each family member's schedule. Use different color ink for each person. Set one day a week when you and your husband synchronize all your calendars. That avoids those embarrassing occasions when each has committed both of you for the same time slot. To keep the peace, make it a policy that neither accepts an engagement without first checking with the other.

Learn to Delegate

Delegate tasks, on the job and at home, whenever you can. If you find this hard to do, examine your thought processes. Perhaps you feel that no one else does it quite as well—and that may be true, especially if the individual is new at it. But will the difference in quality really matter? Give co-workers under your leadership the chance to grow. The job will get done—perhaps not to your standard, true—but you'll be freed to tackle something else.

If you have youngsters, draft them, too. Even very young children can be in charge of setting the table, unloading tableware from the dishwasher, carrying their plates to the sink, etc. Such small tasks teach responsibility in an easy, natural way. Help children form the habit of putting away toys after they play and of tidying the area before bedtime. (You'll probably have to work alongside, at least at first.) In essence, don't do anything for them that they can do for themselves. That's not only for your own self-preservation but also for their development.

Always praise what your children do well and ignore the rest. They'll learn. If you constantly criticize their performance, they'll give up trying. (In fact, if you complain that no one ever volunteers or carries through at your house, you might want to do a bit of soul-searching.) Decide for yourself which has more lasting value—absolutely dustless furniture or your children's sense of contributing to the family enterprise. And don't just ask them to "help"; assign definite tasks with a completion time and then follow through by monitoring.

One family chooses jobs every Saturday. Early risers get first dibs on the job list; sleepyheads are stuck with what's left. (In that home, it's not necessary to nag the kids to get up!)

Set Up Family Guidelines

*I*f your children are old enough to understand, you can adopt as a family principle some guidelines similar to those often posted in church kitchens:

- If you take it out, put it back.
- If you get it dirty, clean it up.
- If you make a mess, clean it up.
- If you turn the light on, turn it off when you're through.
- If you want privileges, demonstrate reliability by doing what's expected of you *without* being reminded.
- You're part of the team; do your fair share.
- Complaining helps no one. Be a good sport.

- Be an encourager.
- Everyone is needed to make this work, so everyone is equally important.

Some working parents regularly pay their children (proportionate to age and ability) for doing household chores. Others pay their kids only for jobs they'd otherwise pay to have done. Probably most parents give a flat allowance and expect everyone to pitch in on whatever needs doing. The choice is yours.

Maximize Your Time

*D*on't be bashful about (calmly) letting people know that you're under time pressure. If you take off work to get Tommy to the orthodontist, tell the receptionist when you come in. That simple statement could save you costly time fuming in the waiting room. And always carry a book to read or a packet of note paper and stamps.

Do you face a long commute to work? Some couples move from the suburbs to the city, saving an hour or more each day. If that's not desirable, examine how you use that commuting time. For example, many people listen to tapes. You can borrow (or rent) tapes of Bible studies, sermons, etc., from various Christian tape-lending services. The entire Bible is available on cassettes. You could master a foreign language, listen to literature classics, or improve your people skills. You can hear famous motivational speakers, learn about time management, brush up on finance. Visit the tape section of your local public library or bookstore. You might be surprised what's available.

If you're a passenger, you're free to read. Bypass the best sellers and nourish your spirit by reading and meditating on the Bible. Or choose from the bountiful array of Christian books.

Since time together as a family is limited, use what you have to reinforce your relationship with your children. This isn't so much a campaign as a pattern of interaction that becomes habit. Let your love show. Speak it. Get in the habit of patting your child's head or shoulder when you walk by. Give lots of quick hugs and kisses. No, this won't become objectionable, because no parent spends all their time at it. As a working mom, your mind is likely preoccupied with holding your double life together, so you'll more easily forget those signs of love, rather than to overdo them.

As another way to express your love, praise the good in your offspring. If you're blessed with "good kids," don't allow yourself to take them for granted. They need your verbal reinforcement, your "warm fuzzies," every bit as much as troublesome youngsters. Develop a listening ear that picks out character traits you want to see developed in your child. Whenever you discern even a hint of that quality, strengthen it by affirming it out loud. Then watch them blossom!

Structure your surroundings, too. Set up an area in your kitchen just for kids. Let there be room to work and materials for projects nearby: construction paper, crayons, scissors, glue, puzzles, play dough, etc. You can buy ends of newspaper rolls cheaply from your local newspaper. While you're preparing dinner, encourage the children to work at their "activity center." (No TV please, it defeats your purpose.) Fix some celery and carrot sticks or apple wedges. Ask the kids to tell you about their day. What did they like? What was fun? Were they sad about anything? Etc.

Then share the details of your own workday. Tell them about the people you work with. Pass on anecdotes; repeat amusing remarks and humorous situations. If you've had a rough day and are feeling impatient, explain why. Reassure them how much you missed them and how glad you are to be able to be home with them because you love them so much.

Make mealtimes count, too. These can be your "communication hours" if you plan for and encourage the whole family to gather. Allow ample time to share; even the smallest child gets a chance. Some families have "table topics"—a subject to discuss over dinner. This can be a news item, something interesting from school, an interesting quote, etc. One family uses the same question every night: "What new thing did you learn today?" Or each person can relate what made them laugh—or think—or feel sad—during the day. Your family style dictates whether you'll have a well-ordered discussion or a verbal free-for-all. Be sure, however, that no one misses a chance to share a hurt or a problem. And institute a firm ground rule: No one is allowed to put down or ridicule another person's experience or emotion. Healthy disagreement with opinions is one thing; personal disparagement is quite another and destructive.

Even when you're going out later on or perhaps are eating at a later hour, sit with your children while they eat. Don't use the time for lectures. Rather, listen—and learn what's going on in their lives. You can't afford not to.

Sometimes what you hear may sting. Perhaps one child had a school play and you weren't there—again. It's okay to say, "I wish I could have seen it. I bet you were terrific!" But don't apologize for being dual-career parents. That's not a crime, just a challenge. And there are benefits for your children, too, as well as inconveniences.

T *Take Advantage of Small Moments*

wo-career couples won't want to overlook opportunities for special time with their children, so be creative. If distance and schedules permit, check with your care giver or your child's school and arrange to eat lunch with your child once a week or so. Share a sack lunch in the park or go out for a hamburger. (If you believe your child's horror stories, it will take courage, but perhaps you could join your child in the school cafeteria.)

Try to have a few minutes alone with each child every day. Read a bedtime story, then linger awhile. Give your child your full attention as you listen to the tortuous clarinet rendition—again. Notice the bouquet of dandelions lovingly presented and use it as a centerpiece. Make a big deal when a child has a good report card or when any family member achieves. Announce it officially. You might blow up some balloons or quickly letter a newsprint banner. ("Way to Go, Marty!" is enough.) Some families keep a special plate to be used by the person with something to celebrate: a birthday, passing a test, learning a new skill, making a sale, etc.

Affirm your child to your friends; *never* tell embarrassing anecdotes or ridicule your children in front of their peers. Let your offspring hear you tell your husband that you're proud of them—and why. Make it your mutual goal that each child feels loved and important. You can accomplish that much more effectively in ordinary ways than by infrequent, expensive outings.

Remember that the connection between parents and child is a sturdy cable, constructed over the years from the delicate filaments of little things—everyday happenings, thoughts, feelings, fears, joys. As you share your life together, those tenuous strands between you strengthen—day by day, little by little.

Enjoy Your Daily Reunion

At the end of your workdays/school days, you gather at home base. People have different names for that period. Some call it "zero hour"; others label it "the witching hour." What you call it depends on your temperament—and probably on whether you have children.

Possibly that's a relaxing time when you and your husband sit down, kick off your shoes, and rejoice that the pressure is off for awhile. For many, however, it's something else. "When I finally get home after picking up the kids, they're hungry and cranky, and I have a headache," says Andrea. "All I want to do is put on a robe and collapse, but I have to pull myself together and get dinner on the table."

You're likely short on patience, and your darling children, having spent the day away from you, now demand your full attention. Some authorities even suggest that kids are extra fussy at this time because they're subconsciously making you pay for "abandoning" them. Youngsters are specialists at knowing which parental "buttons" to push so as to rouse your temper. Beat them at their own game; outmaneuver them. Smile and stay pleasant. Reassure them that you understand how they feel and that you missed them, too. Then tell them what great kids they are to be such good sports. But don't let them get away with manipulating you through your guilt feelings. If they succeed, it can set up destructive habit patterns.

Grown-ups crave the same kind of attention, only they've (we've) been trained to be somewhat more restrained. In the two-income marriage, both partners face their own stresses during the day. Perhaps one partner, seeking consolation, exclaims, "You won't believe what a rotten day I've had! Let me tell you what happened." The spouse, however, may retort, "Don't tell *me* your troubles! My day was no picnic, either!"

Attitude Adjustment

There is a better way. Begin by meeting the most obvious need: hunger. Think of feeding time at the zoo. The ravenous animals are snarling and growling. Kids—and adults—do the same thing during that frantic predinner period. And you're in no mood to be sweet yourself.

Why not institute a family ritual that will calm everyone down and build closeness? Have a daily "wind-down" period when you return from work. Put out some nutritious snacks: cheese spread and whole-grain crackers, carrot and celery sticks, zucchini strips, broccoli buds, cauliflower sections—just about anything can be nibbled with a low-calorie dip made with yogurt instead of sour cream. Or spread peanut butter on celery sticks or apple sections. Trot out something to drink, too. Milk, juice, no-sugar drink mixes, herb tea are all beverages everyone can enjoy.

Get out of your working clothes and into something more comfortable. Then flop on the floor, sprawl on the couch, or sit and put your feet up. Now everyone gets to talk about their day. You'll hear things at this time of the day that won't be shared if you say, "Tell me later when I have time to listen."

Be sure that each family member gets a chance early on to relate something funny or happy. That ensures that each will be on the lookout for positive happenings throughout the day.

As you relax, the stress of your day will ebb away. Allow a half-hour or so to talk and catch up on each other. This is your opportunity to enjoy being a family. (Skip the evening news—you can catch it later.)

Such an interval can make a marked difference in the atmosphere of your home. Sure, you'll have a shorter evening since you'll finish up in the kitchen later. But this oasis in your day can be like letting off the steam in a pressure cooker, so you won't really lose any time. This is strictly a win-win situation.

As another option after work, go for a walk or jog—alone, as a couple, or as a family. Even if you think you couldn't possibly move, you'll find that the exercise will re-energize you.

Structure your late afternoon for mutual pleasure. Remember that your attitude is observed—and copied. So if you respond with temper and impatience when your children whine and squabble, that's what they'll feed back to you.

Don't Overlook Your Marriage Relationship

Sometime during the evening, be sure to save time for you and your husband to talk without interruption. The old saying, "Troubles shared are halved, joys shared are doubled," was never truer in marriage to a caring mate.

The condition, however, is love in action. For example, suppose your husband is depressed or truly worried. He may need to dominate the conversation. Can you put aside your own concerns and just listen with your full attention—without demanding equal time? That's what Jesus would have us do. And it's immeasurably strengthening to your marriage bond when each spouse can demonstrate such practical love and support.

> *This is the message you heard from the beginning: We should love one another. . . . This is how we know what love is: Jesus Christ laid down his life for us. And we ought to lay down our lives for our brothers. . . . Dear children, let us not love with words or tongue but with actions and in truth. . . . Since God so loved us, we also ought to love one another. No one has ever seen God; but if we love one another, God lives in us and his love is made complete in us. . . . We love because he first loved us. (1 John 3:11, 16, 18; 4:11–12, 19)*

Love is more than keeping the peace. Build up each other at every opportunity—and be specific. "I used to tell Ross he wasn't demonstrative enough," says Tammy. "I'd say, 'I feel we don't communicate,' or 'We need to do something interesting on weekends.' But nothing much happened.

"What helped was when we made lists and spelled out what we wanted. For instance, I said I wanted to be hugged and kissed more often, outside our bed—that it would make me feel loved if Ross would compliment me in front of others. And we each wrote down particular activities we wanted to try and places we'd like to explore on weekends. Then we shared our reactions. Ross said it was a relief to know exactly what I wanted.

"Poor guy!" continues Tammy. "Last month he brought me a beautiful bouquet for our anniversary and I said, 'Oh, they're lovely. Too bad they won't last.' When I saw his face, I could have bitten off my tongue! But I had never told him I preferred living plants. On the other hand, when he got a promotion, I bought a helium balloon and put up a 'Congratulations!' banner. *I* thought he'd be tickled pink, but he was home an hour and never even noticed. So we really needed to find out what matters to the other—and what doesn't."

Always, in every marriage, two individuals live with two sets of expectations. Smooth out the rough spots by honestly communicating your wants and needs to each other—with gentleness and sensitivity for the other's feelings. Then comes love with understanding.

Make my joy complete by being like-minded, having the same love, being one in spirit and purpose. . . . Each of you should look not only to your own interests, but also to the interests of others. (Phil. 2:2, 4)

No one else can nurture your marriage relationship. Your mutual commitment and involvement is to your marriage what light and water are to a plant. Without that, your relationship may survive—but it will not grow. To put it another way, if you consider open communication and time with each other critical to your relationship (and they are!), you'll plan for them and block out space in your schedules. There's nothing more important, except your relationship with the Lord.

What Kind of Lover Are You?

*I*t's clear that God loves us, that He supplies love, that Jesus Christ is to be our role model for living in mutual servanthood, and that the Holy Spirit empowers us. The logical questions are *how* and *how will we know*. Here's a short check list that illustrates the answers. You'll probably recognize the basis as you go along.

For self-evaluation, insert your name in the following statement and check the answers that best describe you.

	Usually	Sometimes	Rarely
• _____ is patient	___	___	___
• _____ is kind	___	___	___
• _____ does not envy	___	___	___
• _____ does not boast	___	___	___
• _____ is not conceited	___	___	___
• _____ is considerate	___	___	___
• _____ puts welfare of spouse and marriage before self	___	___	___
• _____ is not easily angered	___	___	___
• _____ keeps no record of wrongs	___	___	___
• _____ shows concern when spouse is troubled or hurt	___	___	___
• _____ rejoices when truth prevails	___	___	___
• _____ always trusts	___	___	___
• _____ always hopes and remains optimistic	___	___	___
• _____ always perseveres, even when the going is rough	___	___	___

- _____'s love and loyalty will never
  fail, no matter what   ___ ___ ___
- _____ is emotionally mature   ___ ___ ___
- _____ possesses faith, hope, and
  love—but especially love   ___ ___ ___

(Based on 1 Cor. 13:4–13)

For those willing to risk being vulnerable, rate each other as well. Then exchange lists and discuss in a spirit of mutual love. Don't allow this exercise to become an exchange of accusations! Each partner needs an attitude that says, "Until I understand how I'm coming across, I can't begin to change. We will support each other, not criticize. We will allow each other the freedom to grow on our own timetable—without reminders. Most of all, we're committed to our marriage!"

Encouragement, Not Condemnation

*I*n case you're feeling thoroughly intimidated by your rating, don't be. No one who's honest could ever have a perfect score. But that checklist does provide a picture of what Jesus meant when He admonished us to love. It's not so much hearts and flowers; it's more like blood, sweat, and tears. Not so much take, but a lot of give. Not as much "I want" as "What do *you* want/need?" Not as much "I need space" as "I need to draw closer to you."

No matter how imperfectly we fit these descriptions, it's the desire of our hearts that counts most. Our Lord already knows that. And if you haven't communicated that deepest longing to your husband, now's the time. When hearts are loving, when we ask the Lord's help in living our lives, when we're determined that our marriage shall not only survive but bloom, then we can—and will—make it work.

The ever-living Christ is here to bless you. The nearer you keep Him, the nearer you will be to one another. (Geoffrey Francis Fisher, Archbishop of Canterbury, at the wedding of Princess Elizabeth) longing to your husband, now's the time. When hearts are loving, when we ask the Lord's help in living our lives, when we're determined that our marriage shall not only survive but bloom, then we can—and will—make it work.

The ever-living Christ is here to bless you. The nearer you keep Him, the nearer you will be to one another. (Geoffrey Francis Fisher, Archbishop of Canterbury, at the wedding of Princess Elizabeth)

The heart of marriage is its communication system. It can be said that the success and happiness of any married pair is measurable in terms of the deepening dialogue which characterizes their union. (Dwight Small)

All I've got to say is: "Be patient" and "Learn to love fast food!" (Husband)

Epilog

Let us not go over the old ground, let us rather prepare for what is to come.
—Marcus Tullius Cicero

Love is not a possession but a growth. The heart is a lamp with just oil enough to burn for an hour and if there be no oil to put in again its light will go out. God's grace is the oil that fills the lamp of love.
—Henry Ward Beecher

It is love that asks, that seeks, that knocks, that finds, and that is faithful to what it finds.
—St. Augustine

Most of the advice directed at harried dual-career couples will bring you up-to-date on the latest systems for coping. But that's like polishing a car on the outside and expecting the engine to run properly as a result.

So it's time to confront the truth—life as it is. To begin with, allow yourself to be human. Nobody is good at everything. Some tasks/activities/memberships may not be worth your time and attention for right now. Stick to what's of value to you and give yourself permission to abandon the rest.

Translate that principle into the responsibilities of running your home. If one task everlastingly keeps appearing on your list of things to be done but never gets done, you might ask yourself whether you truly care. If the answer is "not very much," why keep adding it to your burden?

Realize, too, that relationships will sometimes suffer. For example, you and your husband definitely need time alone on a regular basis. Yet when you go away for a weekend, that's a weekend Mom and Dad do not spend with your children. When you play Super Secretary and put in extra hours to get out a heavy load of work, your boss will be delighted. But your spouse will feel cheated, for some of the time designated "ours" will have been sacrificed to your job.

So don't continue to run the unattainable shoulds and oughts through your mind in an endless accusation. Accept the unalterable fact: That's life. That's the way it is.

You Are Called

*T*here's another unalterable fact that helps us cope: Each of us has a calling from God. You are called to be His child through faith in Christ. Called to be a wife, a mother. (Marriage itself is a calling.) Called to be a bearer of God's light and truth into the job situation. Called to be a giver, without expecting repayment. Called to be a friend to that co-worker who's so unlovable. Called to be a faithful, loyal worker. Called to be a Christian woman who seeks God's guidance and strengthening through faithful, earnest prayer.

As a partner in a dual-career marriage, you're juggling several roles. No one woman can—simultaneously—devote herself fully to husband, children, job, and volunteer organizations. You may be completely committed in your heart, but your body can only be in one place at one time. So keep your priorities straight: (1) wife; (2) mother; (3) employee. Anything else must be fitted in around the edges.

How do you live out your calling as a wife? Does your husband truly feel that he ranks above children and friends? Do you give him your emotional as well as practical support?

Living up to your calling as a Christian means fulfilling your responsibilities. Sometimes that involves hard choices. For example, if you send a sick child off to school, you'll be uneasy all day at work. If you stay home to provide care, you'll wonder how often you can get away with that before you're in trouble with your employer. Either way, you struggle with guilt and pay an emotional price.

In order to have peace of conscience, you must be honest and consistent with your calling. Your child needs reliable care, either from you or from a substitute. Your employer deserves the truth, at the very least. (As a reliable working mother, you'll want to set up a backup system in advance.)

As for outside activities, decide which ones you can manage without shortchanging what comes first in your life. Then give up the rest—at least for a while.

To live a life of Christian integrity, your values and your actions must be congruent with God's Word and His call to you. Otherwise you're on the way to an ulcer or some other stress-related disease. For inconsistency will nag you—and it should.

> Live life, then, with a due sense of responsibility, not as men [and women] who do not know the meaning of life, but as *those who do*. Make the best use of your time, despite all the difficulties of these days. Don't be vague but grasp firmly what you know to be the will of the Lord. . . . And "fit in with" each other, because of your common reverence for Christ. (Eph. 5:15–17, 21 Phillips)

The Continuing Challenge

O rdering one's life by Christian principles has never been easy—and it never will be. Besides our own inner struggles, we're surrounded by inescapable outer influences. Patterns of interaction and thought in our workaday world embed themselves in our consciousness and hook a ride into our private life. We watch television, read newspapers and magazines, and ingest a steady drip-drip-drip of "enlightened opinion." The unrelenting stream is so gentle, so seductively "reasonable," that it can erode our Christian commitment as water eventually wears away stone. The process is so insidious that we likely don't even notice.

If we're to stand firm, we need a solid grip on God's Word.

Then we will no longer be infants, tossed back and forth by the waves, and blown here and there by every wind of teaching and by the cunning and craftiness of men in their deceitful scheming. Instead, speaking the truth in love, we will in all things grow up into him who is the Head, that is, Christ. (Eph. 4:14–15).

Christ, the Head, is the cornerstone of the immovable foundation on which we can rest. Have you come to faith in Jesus Christ as your Savior, who died for all your sins and failures and then rose again (John 3:16; Rom. 10:9)? As His redeemed child, you receive the gift for which the world vainly searches: an inner core of lasting, bedrock serenity.

[Jesus said:] Peace I leave with you; my peace I give you. I do not give to you as the world gives. Do not let your hearts be troubled and do not be afraid. (John 14:27)

We know who we are and whose we are. That knowledge gives us worth as individuals and bestows meaning on our lives, even in the humblest details. When we feel overwhelmed by the constant clamor for our time, our love, and our attention, we do well to recall that it's the Lord Christ we serve, no matter who signs our paychecks (Col. 3:23–24).

It would be lovely to report that Christians have no problems—that the conflict and the time pressure and the perpetually unfinished tasks simply cease to be. That's not, however, true. God has not promised to take away our difficulties; these are often springboards for growth.

He has promised, though, to be with us in our weakness (2 Cor. 12:8–10), to keep us from being overwhelmed (Eph. 6:10–13; Heb. 4:14–16), and to provide all we need (Ps. 103) as we live—and grow—in Him.

When you stop to think about it, what more could we ask?

I urge you to live a life worthy of the calling you have received. Be completely humble and gentle; be patient, bearing with one another in love. Make every effort to keep the unity of the Spirit through the bond of peace. . . . I pray that out of his glorious riches he may strengthen you with power through his Spirit in your inner being, so that Christ may dwell in your hearts through faith. And I pray that you, being rooted and established in love, may have power, together with all the saints, to grasp how wide and long and high and deep is the love of Christ, and to know this love that surpasses knowledge—that you may be filled to the measure of all the fullness of God. . . . And my God will meet all your needs according to his glorious riches in Christ Jesus. (Eph. 4:1–3; 3:16–19; Phil. 4:19)